90 0581138 9

ADHD: A Challenging Journey

Anna Richards

With a foreword by

Geoffrey D Kewley MB BS FRCP FRCPCH FRACP DCH

Lucky Duck is more than a publishing house and training agency. George Robinson and Barbara Maines founded the company in the 1980's when they worked together as a head and psychologist developing innovative strategies to support challenging students.

They have an international reputation for their work on bullying, self-esteem, emotional literacy and many other subjects of interest to the world of education.

George and Barbara have set up a regular news-spot on the website. Twice yearly these items will be printed as a newsletter. If you would like to go on the mailing list to receive this then please contact us:

Lucky Duck Publishing Ltd. 3 Thorndale Mews, Clifton, Bristol, BS8 2HX, UK

Phone: 0044 (0)117 973 2881 e-mail newsletter@luckyduck.co.uk

Fax: 044 (0)117 973 1707 website www.luckyduck.co.uk

ISBN 1 87 3942 84 2

Published by Lucky Duck Publishing Ltd.,
3 Thorndale Mews, Clifton, Bristol BS8 2HX, UK

www.luckyduck.co.uk

Commissioned by George Robinson
Edited by Barbara Maines
Inside designed by Barbara Maines
Cover designed by Helen Weller
Cover photography by Barbara Maines and Ben Robinson
Cover illustration by Philippa Drakeford
Printed in the UK by Antony Rowe Limited

© Anna Richards 2003

All rights reserved. No part of this publication may be reproduced, stored in a retrieval system, or transmitted in any form, or by any means, electronic, mechanical, photocopying, recording or otherwise, without the prior, written permission of the publisher.

The right of the Author to be identified as Author of this work has been asserted by her in accordance with the Copyright, Design and Patents Act, 1988.

Setting the Scene

On the afternoon of Saturday 30th October 1999, Barney Richards, aged 11 and bearer of the condition known as Attention Deficit Hyperactivity Disorder (ADHD), set off with his mother and two of his school friends on a mini-expedition through the English Midlands, which involved train travel, walking and a night in a youth hostel. In the 22-hour period which followed, some remarkable events occurred, which reflect the action-packed and unpredictable lifestyle typical of a child with ADHD.

Multi-faceted and complex, ADHD is considered by Barney's mother, Anna, from many slants – medical, educational, social, criminological and ethical. Peppered with humour, irony, laughter, pain, outrage, discussion and reflection, this journey in space and time is also a journey through the maze of ADHD itself and provides a reader-friendly and thought-provoking introduction to the subject.

Is ADHD merely a middle-class parents' invention and an excuse for poor parenting? Are the children simply naughty and disobedient youngsters, taking well-meaning sympathisers for a ride? Or do they suffer from a genuine neurological condition which makes them, through no fault of their own, difficult to live with, challenging not only to those around them, parents and teachers especially, but also at times to themselves?

Should and can children with ADHD be educated in mainstream schools? Are these youngsters more likely than others to end up in jail? Does giving stimulant medication help them, harm them or interfere with their free will? Why are children with ADHD – and their parents – so misunderstood? Does our society practise 'institutional ADHD-ism'? And how is it possible that, despite their problems, these children end up, in the right circumstances, having so much fun and so many adventures?

These are some of the questions posed in this book. Join Barney, his family and his friends on the journey. Explore some of the possible answers, and expect to be challenged yourself!

About the Author

Born in London in 1953 of Polish and Canadian parents, Anna Richards was educated at Croydon High School. Later, she studied at the Universities of Cambridge, Reading, Cranfield and at Regent College, British Columbia, where she read Natural Sciences, Earth Sciences, Agricultural Engineering and Theology. Her work took her to many parts of England and Africa - to lecture-room, laboratory and field.

Anna is married to Aaron and lives in the English Midlands. They adopted two children in the 1980s – a daughter Laura, and a son, Barney, who has ADHD. For 13 years Anna worked as a full-time parent, snatching spare moments to research ADHD, in order to understand her son better and meet his very complex needs. More recently, she has taken up part-time work as a writer and technical editor. Active in her local church, she also spends time enjoying mountaineering and music, railways and reading, scouting and sport.

University of Plymouth Library
Item No
9005811389
Shelfmark
618.928589RIC

Dedication

This book is dedicated to: Barney, Adam and Lee, with thanks for the gift of one of the most amazing 22 hours of my life; the hapless people who had their lives invaded by ours during this time; my mother, who did the ironing while I wrote this book; Laura, the most loving and understanding sister that we could ever want for Barney; and Aaron, my beloved, faithful husband, friend and companion, who continues to lift me up every time I fall.

Acknowledgement

The author would like to express her heartfelt thanks to all the friends, family and professional people who so generously gave time to read through the first draft manuscript, who criticised so constructively and encouraged so warmly. In addition, the author would like to express immense gratitude to her Local Education Authority who, by the time pen was put to paper in the creation of this book, had come to understand and then acknowledge the very special and complex educational needs which Barney possessed because of his ADHD, and who agreed to place him at an independent school with small class sizes, ample opportunities for physical exercise, and a very practical curriculum, where he is now thriving.

Note

All proper names and identities have been altered to protect the privacy of the people and places mentioned in this book.

Any resemblance between the characters in this book and any living persons is un-coincidental, since the events documented really did occur over the last two days of October 1999. Thoughts and conversations have, however, been expanded for didactic purposes.

The masculine 'he' and 'his' has been used throughout this text because the condition is much more frequently diagnosed in boys than girls at a ratio of 4:1. The behavioural descriptions would apply to both boys and girls.

"Risk more than others think is safe.

Care more than others think is wise.

Dream more than others think is practical.

Expect more than others think is possible." §

Cadet Maxim

§ This symbol, following a quotation, throughout the book, denotes that it was obtained from the internet.

Contents

continued...

# indicates a reference to a term described in the glossary

Foreword

In the past 10 years in the UK, the gap between the knowledge-base about ADHD and clinical practice has widened. One of the reasons for this has been a lack of appreciation of the reality of suffering from, and living with, ADHD and of its impact on the child and family. There has been a very strong tendency to debate over the heads of sufferers. A pseudo-controversy has developed where copious myth and mis-information have been allowed to flourish.

Anna Richards' book is very welcome because it helps get beyond these difficulties. It concentrates on the reality of ADHD and combines first-hand experience of bringing up a child with ADHD with a wealth of information and academic studies. She helps to bring about a better understanding of this condition and brings much-needed information into the public domain in an easy-to-read style and in a unique and extremely effective way. It is always a pleasure listening to those who are not only well informed but who also speak from an understanding of the reality of this distressing condition. I am sure readers will benefit enormously from her book. Whilst giving detailed information about the problems of ADHD, Anna Richards also points out the many strengths and qualities of many children with ADHD.

ADHD is more common than is generally realised, and a thorough knowledge of it is essential if parents and professionals are to help their children effectively. As the knowledge base about ADHD has expanded, the wide range of complications experienced by many children with ADHD is increasingly recognised, as is the fact that these complications may overshadow and obscure the underlying ADHD symptoms. These, and so many other little snippets of information that are only acquired by living with children with ADHD, come through in this book.

This book should be read by professionals and parents alike. It combines a positive understanding of living with a child with ADHD with a great deal of factual information that is essential to the understanding of all those involved in dealing with such children. Much of the myth and mis-information that has hitherto been a problem in the field of ADHD has been caused by a lack of knowledge, by ignorance and mis-information. Anna Richards' book, therefore, furthers the knowledge of this disabling and distressing condition.

Geoffrey D Kewley, MB BS FRCP FRCPCH FRACP DCH
Consultant Paediatrician, Learning, Assessment and Neurocare Centre,
Horsham, West Sussex

Chapter 1

The Journey is Conceived

"Journeys, like artists, are born and not made. A thousand differing circumstances contribute to them, few of them willed or determined by the will – whatever we may think." §

Lawrence Durrell

Before it started I did not know that it would be one of the most intense and action-packed 22 hours of my life. Such a thought never crossed my mind. I can't even remember clearly how the idea of the expedition was first conceived. I think it came about when I suddenly got the urge to take Barney away, to give him lots of special parental attention, with plenty of exercise and a change of scenery. Barney is our 11-year-old son who has, for better or worse, the condition known as ADHD – Attention Deficit Hyperactivity Disorder. It was the half-term holiday. School began again on Monday, so this was our last big chance for lots of fresh air, wide open spaces and togetherness for a while.

Then there was Adam, who also has ADHD. His parents, Edward and Susan, looked washed out and in need of a break. Perhaps if Adam came with us they could get some breathing space. It would be even better with Adam.

So if we were going to take two boys away, I thought, why not make it three and take Lee away too? Lee's mother is a single parent and she might welcome a quiet night. Besides, taking Lee away would mean even more action, more debates, more fun. Five of us – Aaron (my husband), the boys and I would all fit snugly into the car for the return journey.

And so the late-October trip to Tappenham Youth Hostel was born, and in a few days we set off. The idea was that I would leave with the boys after lunch on Saturday 30th October. We would take the train from Babblebrook Railway Station on the Catchley branch line, and travel to Stiltington, where we would walk, via the scenic route, to Tappenham Youth Hostel. Aaron would drive directly to the youth hostel and meet us in time for the evening meal, and Laura, our teenage daughter who preferred not to walk, stay in a youth-hostel, nor spend unnecessary lengths of time with hyperactive, noisy boys, would stay overnight at her grandmother's house.

On the day of departure, Aaron dropped the bombshell.

"I hate to say this... I really hate to say this, but would you mind **very** much if I didn't come?"

"What? Mind? Mind?" I heard myself squawking hysterically. "Why should I mind?... Of course I mind!"

A pained look appeared on my husband's face. "It's just that I've had a really hard week and I'm absolutely knackered."

"Then come and be knackered at the youth hostel!" I retorted sharply. "In fact, I can't think of a nicer place for you to be knackered! All you've got to do is to sit on your backside and have a slow, leisurely drive to Tappenham, to meet us there. It's us who will be doing the walking, not you!"

"I know that, but it's not the walking or the driving that's a problem. It's the rest of the evening, night-time, sheet sleeping bags and a bed that's too short for me."

"Oh come on Aaron! Bring your own bedding if you can't stand the sheet sleeping bag. There's no need to let a minor detail like that spoil your fun."

"Fun?... Look, I'm really tired."

For once I stopped, listened to what he was saying, and took in his whole appearance, not just the grimaces. He was indeed desperately weary. He really did need a good night's sleep and when I thought about it, I knew that, with Barney, Adam and Lee hyped up to the eyeballs with excitement, there would be very little sleep in the dormitory that night. My problem is that when I feel fit, well and energetic I tend to try and sweep others along on my wave of enthusiasm, without examining how they are feeling. Well, Aaron deserved better treatment than this.

"OK," I said. "You stay here. But would you still be willing to collect us at the youth hostel after breakfast tomorrow?"

"No problem!"

Well, that was something to be grateful for, I supposed.

So that left me, all on my own, with three very, very active boys. Never mind. Adventures would surely come our way. With Barney, Adam and Lee it was impossible not to have adventures of one sort or another.

∞ ∞ ∞

Barney, our lovely son, was adopted when he was a tiny baby. He had been born prematurely, weighing only four pounds, and came to us straight from hospital aged 27 days precisely. When he became mobile we did think it was rather unusual that we had to equip his buggy with two sets of harnesses, and his cot with a lid to prevent his Houdini-like escaping acts. But friends (some, not all) and professionals (most, not all) alike told us "He's a boy!" (Yes, thanks for that deeply insightful information – we had actually noticed) and "He'll grow out of it!" (He hasn't) and "It's just a phase!" (A perpetual one). It was not until Barney was eight years old that we got a formal diagnosis of ADHD, and it was such a relief to know, at last, why he behaved as he did.

Adam is just a couple of months younger than Barney and lives a few miles away from us in a neighbouring village. I first got to know Adam when he moved to our area. He was seven and joined the Beaver Scout colony of which I was (and still am) the leader. He won my heart with his gentle nature and his smile. I always knew there was something different about Adam, and something contradictory too. While he clearly had a lovely temperament and went out of his way to seek our approval, the way in which he did this would invariably backfire and, all too often, land him in trouble. Enigmatic to his family and misunderstood at school, the poor lad was not diagnosed with ADHD until he was 11. This meant that he had waited over a decade to get the understanding and help that he so desperately needed, and not for lack of trying by his parents.

Then there is Lee. His mind works as quick as lightning and he can be lethal to argue with. He is highly articulate, but because he has such a sunny personality, his cheekiness is entirely forgivable! Lee is full of energy and is an impressive athlete, gymnast and all-round sportsman. He is very active, and his personality is positively charismatic, but among the three boys who were off to Tappenham, he was the only one not to have been formally diagnosed as having ADHD.

Perhaps that makes him more like me, the fourth member of our group and, because of my age, its leader. I was born in East London in the year during which Queen Elizabeth II was crowned; the cross-bred daughter of a Polish father and a Canadian mother; the unconditionally-accepted wife of long-suffering husband Aaron; and mother (by adoption) of two amazing children, Laura and Barney. As far as I can tell, I do not have ADHD.

Chapter 2

Unpacking the Baggage of ADHD

"...children who are aggressive, defiant, resistant to discipline, excessively emotional or passionate, showing little inhibitory volition, lawless, spiteful, cruel, dishonest, impaired in attention, overactive, prone to accidents, and a greater threat to other children due to aggressiveness. These children display a major, chronic defect in moral control." §

(George F Still, Paediatrician, 1902)

So what exactly is ADHD? I was told of one father who, on hearing the diagnosis that his son had ADHD, wrongly assumed it meant that he, the father, was not giving his son enough attention. Consequently, he supposed, the boy was leaping about all over the place in a hyperactive and disorderly manner to show his parents that he required more attention! This, emphatically, is **not** the meaning of Attention Deficit Hyperactivity Disorder.

It's difficult to describe ADHD adequately without it sounding rather 'text-booky'. If text books are not to your liking, then skip this chapter and go on to the next. You'll pick up the meaning of ADHD from the story anyway. One point may be of interest though; a man in his early 20s who read through the first draft of this book did plough through this chapter and emerged at the other end realising that he himself suffered from Attention Deficit Disorder (without hyperactivity). For the first time, so much that had been puzzling him about his life, made sense.

Gender and activity levels

In ADHD the deficit is that of attention-**paying**, not attention-**receiving** and, like the hyperactivity component, it resides in the 'sufferer' of this condition. Take a typical child with ADHD. Most probably he is a boy – at least four times as many boys than girls are diagnosed with this condition. He is easy to spot. He fidgets, is very active, he 'bounces off the walls' and he is highly impulsive. Barney, when he was younger and before receiving medication, would smash objects and hit other children for no apparent reason, and then not even know why he had done it. The typical boy with ADHD often abandons his seat at the dinner table, at church, on a train, in the classroom or in other situations where remaining seated is expected. He runs and climbs excessively in situations deemed most inappropriate by an on-looking adult, he cannot play quietly and he acts as if driven by a motor. He may talk non-stop, blurt out answers to incomplete questions and interrupt the conversation and games of others. Waiting his turn is almost impossible.

ADHD with and without hyperactivity

Then there is the child with ADD (no 'H') – Attention Deficit Disorder without hyperactivity, sometimes known as '*ADHD Inattentive Type*'. He, or she, tends to day-dream a great deal, sit quietly in a corner, be relatively invisible and therefore go unnoticed in a school setting. Such children are at risk of having their problems ignored completely. Taking both ADHD and ADD children as a whole, approximately 70 per cent are of the first type, that is, hyperactive, while around 30 per cent are of the second type and are not characterised by hyperactivity.[1] It may be, however, that there are vast numbers of girls (and women) who have ADD but are being completely overlooked. Were these females to be accounted for, then the gender ratio of males to females who have ADHD of either type might even approach 1:1.

A child with ADHD, with or without hyperactivity, suffers drastically from an inability to concentrate. He often fails to give close attention to detail or makes careless mistakes in schoolwork or other activities. He exhibits immense difficulty in sustaining attention to tasks or play-activities and rarely seems to listen when spoken to. Frequently he fails to follow through on instructions and fails to finish his chores, duties or schoolwork (if he ever got started in the first place), despite the fact that he has no intellectual difficulty in understanding what he was asked to do, and provided that he isn't setting out to be obstructive.

Tasks which require sustained mental effort, such as schoolwork and homework, are so demanding that he frequently does all he can to avoid engaging in them, or at best, shows great reluctance. He is often forgetful in daily activities and is forever losing the items which are necessary for the task, like toys, tools, pencils, books and school assignments.

Tell-tale signs of ADHD

As the child grows older, one factor begins to dominate his list of special characteristics – that of major disorganisation. One might well argue that if you come across a totally disorganised child it is well worth doing a quick mental check to see if any of the other traits are present and, if they are, giving serious consideration to the possibility that the child has ADD or ADHD. Another 'give-away' sign is that the behaviour exhibited by the child is highly incongruous with his family background, such as when he comes from a home in which parents support behavioural norms and where older siblings demonstrate exemplary behaviour. Alarm-bells should really be ringing if this is the case. Yet the strange truth is that they don't always ring. Many parents become obsessed with the thought *"What did we do to cause this?"*. But why would the younger, difficult child so consistently behave in a way that is so much at odds with his family, with the school and which is so much against his own best interests? Why would he go on generating more and more condemnation when what he desires above all else is everyone's approval? The answer is that either he is unable to help it (a problem or inability to 'self-regulate'), or it is an attempt to cover up what he perceives to be his continual failure in an orderly or academic setting. In the latter case, this failure to be able to give to the adult world what it requires of him is probably not his fault either. It is because he suffers from a condition which, if untreated or unaddressed, is beyond his control.

Neurotransmitters

It is thought that children (and adults) with ADD or ADHD behave as they do because they have a relative shortage of certain neurotransmitters, in particular dopamine and serotonin, in their brain. Recent research shows that the key to hyperactivity seems to hinge on the balance between serotonin and dopamine, and the way they work together in the brain according to the relative levels of each.[2] Neurotransmitters are chemical messengers which are released from one kind of neuron (brain cell) called a pre-synaptic cell and then stimulate the second cell, the post-synaptic cell, across a small gap called a synapse. It does this by attaching to a distinctly shaped area on the neuron, called a receptor site. The union is rather like a key fitting into a lock and triggers signals that either allow the message to be passed onto other cells or that prevent the message from being forwarded. Once the neurotransmitter has done its job, all traces are broken down by a fast working enzyme system. Some scientists think that it may not be so much a problem of **low-level production** of the neurotransmitter, but rather one of the post-synaptic cells **picking up the neurotransmitter less efficiently**. Either way, the person with ADHD experiences an under-functioning of their frontal lobes compared to the majority of the population. This may be why stimulant medication can assist them to concentrate and thereby conform more easily. Research in these areas is going on all the time, and our understanding has to be updated regularly.

Brain scans

I will never forget the first time that Aaron and I saw pictures of the landmark Positron Emission Tomography (PET) scan published by the National Institute of Mental Health (NIMH). This historic image produced by the researcher Adam Zametkin and his colleagues shows the brains of two people, one with and one without ADD/ADHD. Energy generated by glucose metabolism in the frontal lobes was far more concentrated into efficiently burning hot-spots in the non ADD/ADHD person compared to the diffuse, inefficient burning patches within the ADD/ADHD brain. Indeed, we could see the evidence for ourselves, and in my mind's eye I can still see those gloriously technicoloured images – bright orange and yellow fiery centres in the 'ASSes' brain while in that of the 'ADDer', only a few tiny hot-spots surrounded by extensive fuzzy regions of blue and white.

ADDers and ASSes

ADDers? ASSes? What on earth do I mean? Well, it could be argued from the point of view of those who have ADD / ADHD (whom we might refer to as 'ADDers') that the rest of us suffer from 'Attention Surfeit Syndrome' and are therefore 'ASSes'! After all, what the ADDers really have is a brain of alternative design. In their brains, there is relatively little filtering and selection of incoming stimuli, so they are highly distracted by anything and everything which enters ears, eyes, nose, mouth or via their sense of touch. Neural activity is particularly low in the area of the brain which is responsible for attention, motor control and inhibiting responses.

Neuro Developmental Delay (NDD)

Many children with ADHD have comorbid Neuro Developmental Delay (NDD) which makes it particularly difficult for them to sit still for long periods (Comorbid is simply another term for coexisting). NDD is fairly common in children who have been born prematurely or by caesarean section. Such children retain some of the primitive foetal reflexes long after they would be expected to grow out of them – usually within their first year. For example, the so-called Spinal Galant reflex causes a baby to twist from side to side and assists its progress down the birth canal. It is prompted by contact between the baby's lower back and the birth canal itself. It first emerges when the foetus has been developing for around 20 weeks and should be inhibited at some time between three and nine months after the baby is born.[3] We think that Barney still has the remnants of his Spinal Galant reflex. To tell a child who continues to retain this reflex to sit still (when his back is touching a chair) can sometimes be as unreasonable as asking me to stop jerking my foot into the air when my leg is being struck by a rubber hammer just below the knee-cap.

Cuddles and clothing

Some children with ADHD are so sensitive to touch that they do not enjoy being held or cuddled, even when they are babies. When Barney was a toddler he used to become extremely distressed and have emotional outbursts and temper tantrums. Such behaviour baffled us, his parents, and was easily misinterpreted by other adults. Even the labels on clothing or certain textiles can cause a child extreme discomfort.[4] There are plenty of items which Barney has refused to wear after he has been dressed in them and has experienced their 'feel'. I have, over the years, come across several children who persistently remove all their clothes. With hindsight, I can see that they were not necessarily exhibitionists!

Advantages and disadvantages of ADHD

To have ADD/ADHD tendencies can actually be an advantage in certain situations. Such people make excellent hunters and gatherers and, if you and I lived at an earlier stage in human civilisation, these people would be our heroes and heroines, our food-providers, and we would be heavily dependent upon their skills and goodwill for our own survival. As it is, times have moved on, and we 'ASSes' have taken over the world. The danger is that we denigrate and reject the 'ADDers', and, far from being our current heroes and heroines, they are seen as troublemakers, blamed and punished for their difference. Their strong swings of emotion and conviction coupled with extreme impulsiveness do, sadly, predispose them to various kinds of disaster. Many of them have sequencing problems (they find it difficult to report events in an accurate chronological order), and poor short-term memory. Consequently, as has often happened to Adam and Barney, they end up being labelled as liars.

Genetic factors

The genetic influence regarding ADD/ADHD is extremely strong; that is to say, it is highly heritable. Russell Barkley of the University of Massachusetts Medical Center estimates that 40 per cent of ADHD children have a parent with similar symptoms, and 35 per cent have a sibling who is affected too. If one identical twin is affected, the chances are between 80 and 92 per cent that his or her twin will also be affected.[5]

Comorbid conditions

At least 60 per cent of ADHD children have comorbid conditions. These include Oppositional Defiant Disorder (ODD)#, Conduct Disorder (CD)#, Obsessive Compulsive Disorder (OCD)#, anxiety, depression, substance abuse, Asperger's Syndrome# (a form of autism), Tourette's Syndrome#, speech and language problems, coordination difficulties and tics.[6] Moreover, around 30 per cent of children with ADHD (or ADD) have comorbid dyslexia.[#7]

Conditions mimicking ADHD

There are quite a number of conditions which can result in behaviour that mimics ADHD. Sometimes a child may be deaf from time to time. If he is totally deaf all the time it's usually picked up quite early on, but intermittent deafness due to 'glue-ear' may not be recognised. There can be visual problems, the kind of epilepsy known as *petit mal*, learning difficulties, and the effects of child abuse or certain styles of family life. Other conditions which can lead to a child being inattentive, hyperactive, restless, irritable or impulsive include Post-traumatic Stress Disorder (PTSD)# and Attachment Disorder#.

Prevalence of ADHD

It is estimated by American investigators that around three to six per cent of their population is affected by ADHD,[8] while in Britain the condition is reported less frequently, with estimates in the range of 0.5 to five per cent of children affected.[9] It may be that the greater proportion of diagnoses in the States does truly reflect a greater incidence of the condition there. After all, the ancestors of most North Americans today were a self-selected group of high-risk-takers from Europe. These were the people who undertook a hazardous voyage across the ocean, exchanging the fairly predictable and mundane for an exciting new life. It stands to reason that the founding fathers of the USA had a greater than average distribution of ADHD genes in their gene pool.

Whether or not this is so, it is certainly clear that, as we enter the 21st Century, there are relatively few people with ADHD compared with those without the condition – a minority of 'ADDers' surrounded by a vast sea of 'ASSes'. But this wide disparity has probably not always been the case. History shows that in general the 'hunter-type' peoples (the ADDers) of the planet have been dominated, marginalised and even killed off by the better-organised 'farmer-types' (the ASSes). If this is the case, we have a reduced population of ADDers in the world. While killing ADDers is no longer fashionable or legal, I nevertheless see the signs of discrimination, disapproval and even hatred towards them. The characteristics which ADDers display while being morally neutral are invariably described by us ASSes in very negative terms. We regard ADDers as second-class citizens and even pariahs. Observe, in the quotation which introduces this chapter, the way in which the paediatrician George F Still, the first person to document the condition in 1902, viewed it. His words are strong indeed. But like all of us, he was a child of his time and it would be unfair to judge him by today's standards and knowledge. Moreover, it is only fair to remember that words change their meanings over time, and where Still used the word 'moral' some 100 years ago, he would probably use the word 'behavioural' if talking or writing today.

I find that I have even fallen into the negativity trap myself by the kind of language used earlier in describing a child with ADHD; it comes across as pessimistic and disparaging. However hard I try, I know that from time to time this will always be the case. The fact is that I am not an ADDer myself, and while I may sympathise enormously with their differences, I, along with most ASSes, frequently find myself being driven completely mad by their behaviour!

∞ ∞ ∞

A positive presentation of ADHD

Seen from a different perspective, the positive aspect of the ADDers' nature can and should be emphasised more often. For example, ADDers, while seen by ASSes as being distractible are, in fact, constantly monitoring their environment; may be aware of everything; are full of drive and can execute simultaneous multiple thought processes. Many ADDers can even do several things at the same time; are curious and innovative; imaginative and energetic; able to think visually rather than in words; and gifted at solving difficult problems by creating a complete mental picture. Acting without considering the consequences can be seen from a positive perspective as being willing and able to take risks and face danger. While the ASS views the ADDer as being a disorganised, impulsive poor planner, it could be argued that the ADDer is very flexible, adaptable and able to change his strategy quickly. And while the ASS considers the ADDer to be lacking in social graces, the ADDer actually has the virtue of not beating about the bush when decisions have to be made swiftly and then acted upon!

In my experience it is the ADDers, adults and children alike, who are among the most gifted, highly creative, life-affirming and amusing people. Barney frequently has us in stitches! ADDers are well described as being the 'entrepreneurs – the spark-plugs of our society, the movers and shakers, the people who bring about revolution and change'.[10] It is a joy and a privilege to know them, if only we ASSes could take more risks and learn how to understand and get on with them.

Chapter 3

Incarnation

"And the ASS became an ADDer, and dwelt among them..."

(Based on the Gospel of St John, Chapter 1, Verse 14)

It was time to take some risks! Time to let the ADDers loose with the ASS (the one with 'Attention Surfeit Syndrome'). I had to accept that if I, an ASS, was going to be escort to two ADDers plus another live wire, then to function as harmoniously as possible as a team, I would have to be the one to compromise most. I would have to be willing to 'clothe myself' with ADD-type ways of going about things, boldly and unashamedly. I would need to attempt to become the incarnation of an ADDer. For a start, shyness had to be left behind. This strange quality, if we can call it such, is almost unknown to the ADDer. "Don't talk to strangers!" our ASSinine society tells the children. Yet the ADDer-child does not discriminate between strangers and non-strangers. He enjoys striking up a conversation with anyone, wherever and whenever. Very commendable too, I say – at least when his parents are around to keep an eye on him. What richness Barney has brought to our lives by cheerfully addressing the most unsuspecting adults whom he has encountered – even if it was merely to ask them where they were going, or how old they are! The caution we employ to ensure the safety of our children has its drawbacks.

When it comes to my personality I am more introvert than extrovert. I am quite happy being alone, doing things by myself and I even crave solitude. My experience of deliberately taking a risk and abolishing shyness – sometimes with, sometimes without Barney, has paid such dividends in life that I am now rarely tempted to seek cover in its shelter. So, shyness OUT and welcome everybody IN to our lives! OFF with the ASS-fur and ON with the ADDer-skin!

And yet I had to maintain some aspects of being an ASS in order for this escapade to work at all. Take organisation for example. If none of us got organised, we would be unlikely to end up anywhere of consequence. In fact, we would be unlikely to end up together, anywhere at all. If I did not organise getting the train time-table information and act upon it, we would never end up at Stiltington and we would not get to Tappenham tonight.

The amazing thing about Incarnation – for that is what this ASS was proposing, to incarnate as ADDer – is that, contrary to what our common sense at first sight might tell us, it is possible to be two different kinds of entity simultaneously. For example, I have been a daughter all my life, but in 1985 I also became a mother. When I took on this new persona of 'mother', I did not cease to be a daughter. I maintain, to this day, both motherhood and daughterhood simultaneously, without tearing myself in two or becoming a split personality.

The challenge now was to let myself become, insofar as I could manage it, an ADDer for a day, while not ceasing to be an ASS. But could it be done? Read on!

Chapter 4

Immoral? Illegal? Dangerous? Destructive?

"Don't throw away your friendship with your teenager over behaviour that has no great moral significance. There will be plenty of real issues that require you to stand like a rock. Save your big guns for those crucial confrontations." §

(Dr. James Dobson)

"Bee-beep, bee-beep, bee-beep!" The alarm on my wrist-watch interrupted my thoughts and brought me back to where I needed to be – in the kitchen and reaching for the medication box where Barney's Ritalin tablets were kept. Time for his second 10 milligramme tablet of the day.

"Barney, Ritalin time." I called, and made my way towards him in the dining-room.

"Barney, Open up, please." No response. The 11 year old scallywag sat transfixed to the computer screen, his fingers tapping away at the keyboard, completely focussed upon the game.

"Barney! Ritalin time!" Still no response.

This is one of the paradoxical things about ADHD. One minute you are convinced the child cannot concentrate on anything at all for more than a few seconds, and then something as trivial (to me) as a computer game can be so engrossing that the whole house could be burning down around him and he would only notice, or bother to change his occupation, when the flames burned through the electricity supply.

"BAR-NEY!" I bellowed at him. Nothing. I waved my hands between his eyes and the screen. He pushed them aside, rapidly, as though they were merely a pair of inanimate, irritating objects totally unrelated to another human being. I increased the rate and volume of my verbal delivery.

"BARNEY! RITALIN! NOW!"

"Wait!", he wailed. A response at last. Heaven be praised!

"It can't wait, sonny! Open your mouth! Now!" That's it, I thought: simple, clear instructions. That's all that's necessary with a child like this. Miraculously, this time it worked. Barney opened his mouth like a fish, crunched the pill twice and swallowed. No water. Impressive.

If he did not have the Ritalin to help him concentrate, then he might well be swinging from the luggage racks later that afternoon. Right now he was just as engrossed in the computer game as he was before he had robotically consumed the tablet. The term 'Attention Deficit' for these children is a bit of a misnomer. It is more accurate to describe the condition as one of extreme attention variability. We ASSes have, for whatever reasons, decided that predictability is good and unpredictability is bad. Because we form the majority we run our society along these lines. We berate the erratic arrival of London buses at our bus-stop and call it scandalous. Similarly, the wild swings in Barney's attention span cause alarm to us more predictable types, and we label it a 'disorder'.

Much of the predictability which is idolised by us ASSes could be viewed by an ADDer as "Boring! Boring! Boring!". After all, provided that we are fed, clothed, housed and entertained, why should predictability matter so much and what is its merit?

Now that is the thing about these ADDers. They really make you re-think your whole ethical system. This is no bad thing, as it helps us to weed out the extraneous and leaves us with a simpler, leaner morality system. I have found that parenting Barney has challenged my whole system of values. I have found it necessary to be able to integrate what I have learned from him with my own system of values and beliefs. This process has taken time, and continues. It can cause major discomfort. Any parent, carer or teacher who does not manage to reconcile their understanding of ADHD with their own faith (if they have one) and personal value-system will be like a ship drifting around in the ocean with neither engine nor rudder.

Although it is a cool autumn day and the central heating is on, the upstairs doors are open. My mother brought me up to keep doors shut in the colder months – there is no point in heating the bedrooms. However, I have since learned that keeping bedroom doors shut does not have to be a rule in this house. Closing the bedroom doors after Barney had left them open was slowly, but surely, driving me insane. I tried calm, peaceful, smiling good example, taking great care to demonstrate in front of him how to close the door, and explaining the reasoning behind it. But no matter what threats, no matter what promises, no matter what sanctions were placed before Barney, it made no difference whatsoever – he never managed to shut the bedroom door.

In the end I realised that whether or not it was a case of 'He **could** not learn' or 'He **would** not learn', the fact was that he **did** not learn.

How needlessly we impose rules upon our families so much of the time. The art of surviving life with an ADDer son if one is an ASS mother is to keep the number of rules to an absolute minimum, and only bother to have a rule at all if it is a matter of actual morality. All sorts of stupid rules and regulations have been abolished since Barney arrived on the scene. For example, "Thou shalt only eat mint sauce when it is accompanied by roast lamb." Rubbish! Eat it with whatever you like. And "Thou shalt not take a biscuit or chocolate from the bottom layer of the box when there still remains a biscuit or chocolate on the top layer." No. Go for the one you want every time, provided that you are not knowingly depriving another person of their favourite (the ethical component), and enjoy it!

As a result of the richness of challenging experiences gained through having Barney as our son, I knew that the wisest decision regarding 'rules' for our trip to Tappenham was to keep them to the barest minimum. In fact, there would be just four criteria to govern our behaviour. An act would only be forbidden if it was:

1. immoral
2. illegal
3. dangerous
4. destructive.

With these provisos, anything goes!

Chapter 5

Babblebrook Station – The Rules Established

"If you obey all the rules, you miss all the fun." §

(Katharine Hepburn)

Did I say 'anything goes'? Well, I'd like to amend that slightly. I'm going to add another rule to the list... instant obedience!

The doorbell has just rung and the dog is barking like mad and leaping around excitedly. Adam has arrived. Barney has just opened the door and boys, bags and dog are all tangled up in a wriggling heap together on the floor, blocking the hallway. I tell Barney to put his jacket on. The jacket which I have selected is rejected by him in no uncertain terms.

We have just performed another of our several-times-daily rituals of the type which drive many parents, and those whose children have ADD or ADHD in particular, to distraction. Child rejects jacket...goes and selects another jacket...puts it on...finds jacket not to his liking for reasons totally mysterious to the spectator, and rips that one off...dumps it on the floor. For the first time he notices the sweater which he is wearing underneath, decides there is no way he wants to have this one on, rips sweater off and also dumps that on the floor.

Boy ignores mother's appeal to clear up mess and whizzes off upstairs to find another sweater (not needing to open bedroom door in the process since we have all now trained ourselves to leave them open). He does not use memory recall system in brain, if indeed there exists such a system, and therefore not knowing which drawer or cupboard houses the sweater, picks a drawer at random and rifles through it. Boy fails to find sweater, leaves drawer open, and tries another one...

Sod's Law is operating at its best and drawer after drawer fails to reveal the desired garment. Eventually every orifice in every piece of furniture is open and sprawling its contents. Mother realises that the beloved sweater is, in fact, in the wash...

Mother tries to keep calm by looking on the bright side and telling herself that if burglars were to turn up now, they would at least think that other thieves had got there first, so they would beat a hasty retreat! Mother deeply regrets not having left enough contingency time, yet again, since the 13.13 hours departure from Babblebrook Station will wait for no-one.

"Come on boys. We have to go. NOW!"

Somehow I managed to get both boys, all three rucksacks and myself on the outside of the front door, and the dog on the inside. I was sorry that Aaron and Laura (who were out at the time) would come home and find the house in such a state, but what was new? And what choice did I have? To clear up would almost certainly be counter-productive, since policing Barney to tidy such a disorganised bedroom would use up more than a whole day's worth of my patience. I am well aware just how much this sounds like a parental cop-out, but it has to be remembered that organisational skills present a genuine neurological difficulty for ADDers like Barney. To do the tidying up myself would leave Barney on the loose to create even more chaos in another part of the house. This summarises life in the ADHD home fairly well. Does this sound tedious? Well it is. Very. Somehow one is always left, as the adult, thinking that one really ought to be able to do better than this and next time one will do better, but in the meantime it is simply too tiring to change the situation.

∞ ∞ ∞

Moral dilemmas: innocent or guilty?

These are the moral dilemmas which face every parent of an ADDer child almost every day. Is the child genuinely disabled in terms of carrying out our requests, or is he simply being obstreperous and testing the limits? It has been said "ADHDs are unable: EBDs are unwilling" (EBD stands for Emotional and Behavioural Difficulties). But the distinction between ADHDs and EBDs is not always clear in practice. Children with ADD/ADHD (ADDers) usually do have difficulty carrying out the task which they are failing to execute. If they do not have genuine difficulties then, by definition, they do not suffer from ADHD. The question is 'are they really totally unable to do as we ask in these situations?'. If so, they are therefore worthy of our utmost sympathy and assistance. In this case blame and punishment from their carers would be cruel and immoral responses. Yet at the same time, ADDers are human beings capable of making moral choices and choosing to disobey at times. Probably the truth lies somewhere in the grey zone between 'not responsible and thus innocent' and 'totally responsible and therefore culpable'.

With Barney I have come to the conclusion that frequently a task really is difficult for him, whereas to his ASS peers it would be straightforward. His difficulty stems from the extraordinary mental effort which he has to expend to organise his thoughts and actions in order to obey a command. It is rather like someone asking me to get ready to swim across the English Channel and then demanding that I do it. Is it any wonder that I might refuse to comply? If I said "No" and flatly declined, I would be considered as disobedient, unco-operative and oppositional, if I had the misfortune to be part of a society where such feats were common expectation. The request would come across to me as unrealistic, unnecessary and annoying. I think that is how it is for Barney and other ADDers when faced with what we consider to be routine requests. Anyone who has ever suffered from clinical depression or migraine will understand how much effort it takes to carry out what would normally be the simplest of tasks. In both these conditions there is a problem with neurotransmitter functioning, just as there is in ADHD. We must be sympathetic to the aversions and refusals of all ADDers. We will always be left wondering if we are being taken for a ride. Sometimes we will be pretty sure that the child is being deliberately awkward so we will continue with threats, promises and discipline like any other parent towards a recalcitrant child. But we may well end up having to eat humble pie, while compromising and apologising in the process.

∞ ∞ ∞

Barney, Adam and I ran and walked down the hill to the house where Lee lived. His Mum's friend was going to give us a lift to Babblebrook station. At least this part of the proceedings went smoothly and we found ourselves the only travellers waiting on the platform at Babblebrook station on the Cotford to Catchley branch line.

We placed our rucksacks on the red metal bench. I took out some cereal bars and chocolate. We had some serious marching to do later, and an army marches on its stomach. "Munch now, march later!" was our motto, so we tucked in. Morale, which was already high, rose even further.

"Okay boys," I said, in sergeant-majorly style, "there are just two rules that you need to know for this expedition." (I had decided to keep things simple.)

"Rule number one: if I ask any of you to do something there's to be instant obedience. Remember, I'll only ask you to do something if there's a very good reason and the sooner you obey, the better it'll be for all of us.

Rule number two: avoid using the phrase 'It's not fair!' If anyone says this, we set up a kind of court case and put them on trial and the other three of us take a vote on whether 'it' is fair or not. OK?"

"But," started Adam, "that's not ..." and he checked himself abruptly.

"Great!" said Lee. "I want to be a lawyer when I grow up."

It was for this reason that I had introduced rule number two. Lee was a brilliant debater and his cheeky, mock-innocent expressions always caused me a great deal of hilarity. Rule number two existed purely for entertainment.

Two of the quaint things about Babblebrook railway station are the hand-operated level crossing gates and the Thomas the Tank Engine type signals positioned alongside the track, some distance up the line. The signalman appeared from the signal box and shut the gates, one by one. Shortly after he returned to his box the old-fashioned signal, some hundred yards or so off, was raised.

"Train! Train! There's the train!" went the cry and our combined excitement reached fever pitch as the old diesel engine ground to a halt. All four of us seemed simultaneously to squeeze through the narrow door and land, with a 'plop', on the seats.

Chapter 6

On the Train – Babblebrook to Catchley

"Let the train take the strain."

(British Rail advertising slogan, 1970 onwards)

The train pulled away with a jerk and I wondered whether we were the only occupants of the carriage. No, we were not. In a nearby section sat a girl – a young lady to be more accurate. She had been the only passenger in this part of the train before our rude entry. Lee, on spotting her, immediately vacated his original seat and set off to join her. He plonked himself directly beside her.

"Hello, how are you?" he asked, boldly.

The girl smiled, then giggled coyly. "OK."

"My name's Lee. How old are you?"

"Seventeen." More giggles. At least she doesn't look in the least bit intimidated, I thought.

Lee continued to chat her up, totally confidently. Only 11 years of age, testosterone had already started to ooze out of every pore and all good-looking young women whom he encountered caused his eyeballs to roll in ecstasy. Barney and Adam kept away. They could not even begin to match Lee's sophistication at this game. Barney in particular seemed extremely immature for his 11 years. Behaviourally, he was more like a seven-year-old. Sometimes he seemed even younger – three or even four. This is very typical of a child with ADHD. The text-books warn you to expect a behavioural age of around two-thirds of the child's chronological age, and most of the time I think this is an accurate estimate for Barney. Physically too, Barney was noticeably smaller than most of his peers. Well-proportioned, his wiry body bore no traces of surplus fat. In fact, it was difficult to find any fat on him at all. His leanness could well be explained by his high level of physical activity, but his small stature was less easy to account for. Perhaps his natural parents had simply been short. Whatever the reason, it was apparently very common for children with ADHD to be small for their age.

Some people attribute this to the side-effects of Ritalin medication. While it is true that Ritalin can suppress the appetite, the child usually makes up for lost eating time at the end of every day when the last tablet has been metabolised and his system is virtually Ritalin-free. This certainly was the case for Barney, who would frequently show great reluctance to eat during the long hours between breakfast and around nine o'clock at night, but would then sit down to pack away course after course of very high calorie food.

It was not as if he had ever been average or large for his age before he was prescribed Ritalin, beginning shortly after his eighth birthday. He had always been small. Then

there was Rory, another boy with ADHD, who lived in our town. Rory was 15 years old before he was diagnosed as having ADHD, after which he started taking Ritalin.
He, like Barney, was small and way behind his peers in both physical and behavioural maturity. It seems a characteristic of the condition and cannot reasonably be blamed on the medication. How envied will Barney and Rory be when they reach the ripe old age of 90 and they look and behave like 60-year-olds!

The train slowed to a halt. The young girl got out, probably greatly relieved. Was it only coincidence, I wondered, that she had escaped us at the very first station possible? We still had seven stops before we reached Catchley on this charming branch line. The three boys spent the rest of this part of the journey leaping around from seat to seat – landing with bottoms and not with feet, I hasten to add. They were having a whale of a time. Somewhere between Arrowhill and Catchley, Barney and Adam landed simultaneously side-by-side as if from a great height on one particular seat, sending a huge plume of dust cascading upwards towards the ceiling. We all shrieked with laughter.

For the entire stretch of rail between Babblebrook and Catchley, nobody chose to enter our carriage.

Chapter 7

Catchley Station and the Bellowing Killjoy

"Living at risk is jumping off a cliff and building your wings on the way down." §

(Ray Bradbury)

One of the big advantages of Catchley station compared to Babblebrook from the boys' point of view was the presence of multiple railway tracks and many platforms. Some means of connecting the platforms was needed and this meant bridges and steps. Wow! What an opportunity for some fun. We had 15 minutes to 'kill' before the Stiltington train would arrive on the main line. Barney, Adam and Lee had no problem in finding something to do. In fact it could reasonably be said that they exhibited giftedness in amusing themselves without my assistance. No whining from them. No wails of "We're bored. What can we do?" They knew exactly what they wanted to do, so they went straight ahead and got on with it.

Their amusement consisted of that old, old pastime of sliding down the banisters, or rather, the railway equivalent. Dividing the staircase, which descended from the connecting bridge to the area between Platforms 4 and 5, was an inviting, white, metal handrail. Starting at the top each boy took it in turns to propel himself off in a manner which would have done the Jamaican bobsleigh team proud. Muscular energy transmuted into kinetic energy, which increased in proportion to the ever-decreasing potential energy, resulting in a truly spectacular final velocity and launch along the length of the platform. What was equally impressive was the variety of styles which they devised. Barney favoured the classic straddle – one leg either side of the rail, chest and belly in contact with the metal. Adam seemed to prefer a transverse technique – rail running across his body, higher on his left, lower on the right, head down, doubled over, as if he had been struck in the solar plexus. Lee, most impressive of all, rode side-saddle, displaying a wonderful sense of balance.

Every descent was accompanied by whoops of a "*Ride 'em cowboy!*" variety. It was rare for one boy to reach the bottom before another had already begun a new descent. Their joy and thrills seemed to know no bounds. I considered having a go myself, but so engaging was the spectacle, I rapidly concluded that I would get more pleasure by treating it as a spectator sport.

∞ ∞ ∞

Physical Restrictions

How desperately children need to let off steam, particularly after they have been cooped up in a railway carriage for 26 minutes, and especially if they have ADHD.

Opportunities to do this seem to be fewer and fewer these days, especially at school. I remember that when I was at school we either had games (outdoors in all kinds of weather) or gymnastics (indoors) every single day. For Barney and Lee there was no such luxury. They were attending their local mainstream school which seemed to adhere to the National Curriculum very closely. Those who plan the curriculum seem to have forgotten that human beings have bodies attached to their brains so physical exercise only takes place for two hours a week. Even though this local school has ample indoor and outdoor play areas, of the kind which most inner city schools can only dream of, there are very few sporting opportunities on offer apart from the statutory two hours' worth of lessons. Whatever happened to the idea of *mens sana in corpore sano* – a healthy mind in a healthy body?

Many children today suffer from physical restriction in school, at home and in the community. Not only have the hours of physical exercise lessons been cut at school, but parents coop them up at home, refusing to let them play out, run around, explore their environment, afraid of what might happen to them. Unfortunately this culture of fear has now become so pervasive that few parents let children play out. And because these children are now in the minority, they no longer have the same level of protection from one another in case of accident or mishap. The mutual surveillance system of yesteryear is no more.

According to Home Office statistics, children are far more likely to be killed by their parents or carers than by strangers. An average of 78 children were murdered each year in England and Wales between 1984 and 1994, but nine out of 10 of them were murdered by parents, carers or others close to the child. Public concern tends to focus on child murders by strangers, but children, like all victims, are most likely to come to harm from people known to them.[11]

If Barney was asked what he liked best about school he would answer "Playtime". The only exception to this was when he replied "P.E." or even "Going home"! Everything he liked best was physical. This is very common among children with ADHD. They need to move. They crave action. Their problem with sustained concentration often leads to learning difficulties and failure to complete the task set during the lesson-time. What happens next? They are forced to spend the break time staying in to catch up on the work. The very children for whom exercise is a necessity are penalised by the withdrawal of this opportunity. In some cases this is a great hardship – even cruelty. Yet it is probably rare that the teacher involved means to be unkind. Far more likely he or she simply does not understand what lies behind the child's failure to complete his work. Making teachers and all school staff more aware of ADHD in all its manifestations and complexity is vital if these children are to be free from this kind of mis-management.

Discrimination

The reduction of gymnastic and sporting opportunities in many schools may also discriminate against children with ADHD in other ways too. Many of these children are not necessarily academic high-fliers, but may be gifted at gym or at a particular game. Here is the one area in the curriculum where they can really succeed, where they can make a public, positive contribution to their school, and where they can experience the positive effects of having their self-esteem raised.

When P.E. lessons do actually take place, it is ironic that yet another form of subtle discrimination against ADDers frequently occurs. Because of the organisational problems, it is common for these children to appear at P.E. lessons without some vital piece of clothing or equipment. Many P.E. teachers make it a rule that any child who fails to come properly equipped is forbidden to participate. The teachers claim that they have to have one rule for all but this fails to take account of the neurological nature of the child's problem. ADDer children are different, even though this is not apparent from their physical appearance. In being refused access to the P.E. lesson, they are discriminated against on account of their disability.

The three 'R's and the three 'F's

In the classroom, while other children are making great strides forward with the three 'R's (Reading, wRiting and aRithmetic), the children with ADD and ADHD are repeated victims of the three 'F's (Fear, Frustration and Failure). Is it any wonder that school becomes an increasing nightmare for them, or that their behaviour deteriorates? Unless the underlying ADD/ADHD is diagnosed, understood and addressed, ADHD can, slowly but surely, evolve into EBD (Emotional and Behavioural Difficulties).

∞ ∞ ∞

Slowly I distanced myself from the shrieking boys and considered the four criteria which I had decided to apply as arbiters to decide whether the boys' activity was acceptable – Immoral; Illegal; Dangerous; Destructive. Was whizzing down the handrail immoral? Definitely not. So OK on the first point. Was it illegal? Well, I am sure that according to the law of the land it is a perfectly legal pursuit. As for the 'house-rules' of the station, there was no evidence or notice to tell me that they were being broken. So, OK on the second point too. Thirdly, is it dangerous? Aah, this one is a little less simple. "Is it dangerous?" Certainly it was not as dangerous as it looked. These boys are masters in the art of self-preservation. They are very skilled at what they are doing. Barney and Adam are probably significantly safer descending the stairs via the hand-rail than the more conventional passengers who descend the stairs on foot. As for Lee, his sense of balance is so good that he really is in very little danger. There is risk. Of course there is some risk. In fact it is probably the element of risk which makes the whole enterprise so thrilling. There is a necessary but acceptable level of risk. OK for point number three part 'a' then, is it dangerous for them? Point number three part 'b' asks "Is it dangerous for other people? Are the boys posing a danger to the other station users?" The answer? Most definitely not! No-one is going near them! Everyone is giving them a very wide berth, and even the few people who do have to use the staircase are having no problem plastering themselves against the walls at the side and ascending or descending like crabs. So, no problem here, either.

What about part four? Is it destructive? No. The metal rail is very strong and is very firmly secured. There is no possibility of the boys destroying the handrail. Or is there...? I suppose, there is a remote possibility that the rail might break. If that happens, then the boys will, in fact, be heroes, preventing the breakage from happening on a later occasion when some frail old lady might have been relying on it for support. In fact, one might reasonably argue that the boys were doing a great service to the Catchley station users by testing the handrail without seeking financial reward from the Health and Safety Executive! So point number four was OK too.

I did have to admit, rather grudgingly, that the boys were making an awful lot of noise. So, should I stop them on these grounds? Well, think about it. How many decibels were they actually producing? I did not know as I had not brought a sound-meter with me. But one thing was certain. The passing high-speed trains which were thundering through the station were generating a great deal more noise than these charming playmates. So, let the children play!

Before long, my satisfactory, silent verdict was horribly interrupted by one of the most unpleasant sounds I had heard in a long, long time.

"What the b* * * * * h * * * do you think you're doing? Get down **now** and pack that up, d'ya hear me, else you'll be in real trouble!"

A uniformed official, from one of the many railway companies, vented his wrath at top volume, drowning out the squeaks of the three boys. Esther Rantzen would have undoubtedly called him a 'jobsworth'. I silently named him 'The Bellowing Killjoy'. It had obviously not occurred to him that Barney, Adam and Lee were in the charge of any adult and it was clear that The Bellowing Killjoy would not be in a receptive mood to be lectured by me about 'play-theory' or the needs of children with ADHD. Maybe I had to concede that accepting noisy, dynamic kids as having a legitimate place in the public arena was simply not part of the British culture. In fact, most of the objections made by the general public in this country about the behaviour of ADDer children centre around cultural rather than moral unacceptance.

The boys scattered and, by various routes, eventually found their way to me.

"Sorry, kids," I said – not as an apology, but rather as a true expression of my sorrow and commiserations. "And I'm sorry that I'm going to have to make another rule – keep behind this yellow line, and that one on Platform 5 as well, until our train has stopped. I don't want you getting sucked underneath a passing loco".

Barney and Lee continued to leap along the platform. Adam seemed pensive.

"In the olden days," he reflected, "boys used to have fun."

"Yes, Adam, they did, and I don't see any reason why they still shouldn't have fun."

"In the olden days," he continued, "they used to put pennies on the railway lines to make them go flat when a train came along."

"Barney's Dad used to do that when he was a boy," I mused, "but the difference between most of the trains then and some of the trains now is one of speed. If you tried getting on that line with a penny today, then instead of a nice flat penny, we'd probably end up with a poor, pancaked boy!"

Our train arrived. The doors opened automatically. The boys gleefully stepped over the yellow line and leapt in.

Chapter 8

On the Train – Catchley to Stiltington

"Life is either a daring adventure, or nothing." §

(Helen Keller)

Snuggled next to her bag she sat, the only other passenger in our carriage. She was big and black. Her eyes were twinkling kindly and her ample bosom strained at the buttons of her grey woollen coat. Lee instinctively sat down directly opposite her, pointedly ignoring row upon row of empty seats whose delights Barney and Adam had already begun to explore.

"Hello! May I keep you company?" he asked openly.

"Of course!" she replied, the letter 'r' pronounced high up in the roof of her palate, betraying her Caribbean origins.

"Where do you come from?" Lee continued his interrogation.

"From Jamaica, an' I'm goin' to London to see my daughter," she replied, smiling warmly and welcoming his sincerity and interest in her.

"My mother comes from Jamaica!" exclaimed Lee with pride. They chatted on in a very relaxed maternal/filial style and, with the other two boys preoccupied some way away, I turned again to my own thoughts.

∞ ∞ ∞

I was still feeling a slight emotional back-lash from the Bellowing Killjoy experience. It had all been so harsh and so unnecessary. Yet I managed, from somewhere within me, to find some sympathy for the old curmudgeon. He was a product of our times and our society, and he might well have been accused by his employers of failing in his duty if he had not reprimanded the boys. There was a vast gap between our different philosophies. He just did not see that these active boys were actually much safer on the staircase than had they been anywhere near the platform edge.

On another occasion, at Gatwick Airport railway station, Barney had generated an 'incident' on the train rails when he had inadvertently (in his bang-crash-rush manner) dropped a bag onto the line. This bag had fallen through the gap between the platform edge and the carriage floor of the train when we were boarding. Consequently we had to let that train go without us and draw the attention of the railway official to our plight. We showed the uniformed man where the bag was and he said he would remove it for us when he had a moment. He then proceeded to ignore us and our situation in a manner which strongly suggested that he was trying to punish us in some way.

Meanwhile, Barney began to relieve his boredom by running up and down the escalator. I was grateful for this diversion. He was having a wonderful time, and I admired his repeated achievement of running down the 'up' escalator. The physical contact which his feet were having with the contraption was no greater than that of a standard user, and in no way was he being a significant danger to himself or others. Nobody else was using the escalator at the time and this moving staircase was keeping Barney well away from any danger at the platform edge. Unfortunately, our peak-capped friend did not see things in the same way and not only cautioned Barney loudly but also brought to an end the source of his fun by pulling a red handle which disconnected the electricity supply and stopped the escalator. I think it was at this point that the man realised that he had been punishing himself far more than he had been punishing us. He got a long pole with a hook on the end and retrieved the bag. He had learned what I had long ago discovered; when we try to punish a child with ADHD, it invariably back-fires on us and we end up far more exasperated and frustrated.

We adults end up punishing ourselves when we try to encourage our ADHD children to carry out various domestic chores and responsibilities. For example, when Barney was about six years old I made it clear to him one day that it was his turn to wash up after tea. He had surely seen what to do over the preceding years and I had given him a head-start by filling the sink with hot water and washing-up liquid. I also filled a small bowl on the draining board with hot water for him to rinse the dishes in before he placed them in the rack a little further to his left. Together, we cleared the table and stacked the dirty plates on the right-hand side of the sink. I said to my son,

"OK Barney. You know what to do, don't you? Just put the dirty dishes into the hot soapy water, brush them clean, rinse them in the bowl and place them in the rack. See how many you can get done before I get back."

Then I made the mistake of leaving the room.

When I returned a couple of minutes later, the neatly stacked plates were now in collapsed heaps, some on the floor. Barney was sitting in the sink, in the hot water, fully clothed and surrounded by bubbles. Water had overflowed onto the floor. If he had even one plate in the sink with him it would have signified some kind of progress but, alas, there was not even one. My attempt at training him to pull his weight in our household and contribute towards mealtime tasks had completely failed. By the time I sorted out the mess I was exhausted and demoralised.

We parents of ADDer children live on 'permanent red alert'. It saps our energy and eats away at our stamina. Our only relief comes when some other, wonderful, person whom we trust implicitly, takes care of our child so that we get a break – better still, a holiday.

∞ ∞ ∞

Loud cackling from Barney and Adam who were up to something jerked me back to the present. Outside the window the English countryside sailed by at a clickety-clack pace. The train decelerated with a protracted whine as we approached Stiltington.

"Come on boys! It's our station. Don't forget your rucksacks. Come on over to this door you two."

Barney and Adam stumbled, sparred and giggled as they made their way over to the rest of us. Lee waved a fond farewell to his Jamaican friend and once again we landed in a heap on a platform, as if disgorged by a relieved train whose hissing door simulated a gentle sigh.

Chapter 9

An Unintentional Rejection

"If you can keep your head when all about you are losing theirs, it's just possible you haven't grasped the situation." §

(Jean Kerr)

"Where are we?" asked Adam as I battled with a non-compliant Ordnance Survey map, caught by a passing gust of wind.

"Er, just here. See that red blob, where it says Stiltington Station? We're there, just coming up the white track onto that yellow road. The road's not really yellow, Adam, as I'm sure you know. It means that it's a minor road. That brown one marked there corresponds to the main road over there. See? The really busy main roads are marked in red. Fortunately we don't have to go anywhere near them."

Lee came up to look at the map too, with Barney closely in tow.

"So where are we going then?" asked Lee.

"A good question!" I replied. "And the answer depends on the timescale. In the long run we're going down here...See that red triangle in the middle of that village? That's Tappenham Youth Hostel. But we're not going to walk straight there. In fact, we're going to go this way, along this footpath and bridleway, 180 degrees off course – the scenic route."

"Why?" asked Adam, as Barney buzzed around us, kicking at any and every object on the ground around his feet – stones, leaves, beech-nut cases, bottle tops, and the occasional chocolate bar wrapper or aluminium can.

"For two reasons. Firstly, if we go direct we'll get to the hostel a long time before it opens, and we'll get cold and fed up hanging around outside. Much better to keep warm by walking. And secondly – BARNEY! GET OFF THE ROAD! (yank) – where was I? Oh yes, secondly, if we take this longer, more scenic route, not only do we avoid roads and enjoy the traffic-free footpaths and bridleways, but also we have a delightful walk alongside this blue-ribbon thing. Here, look! Do you know what that blue wobbly line represents? – BARNEY! MOVE! YOU'LL GET RUN OVER!" (yank).

"It's a river," said Adam.

"Close," I replied. "A canal actually. What you might call a man-made river. Lee, do you know what that little black arrow means?" Adam and Lee tried to pull the map open further, to see the key, and the map became even more unwieldy.

"I think I'd better tell you." I wrestled further with the undulating sheet and got it under control. "It's a lock, with lock gates. So if you'd looked in the key, you would have found a lock! It's usually the other way round." I quipped.

"O ha ha!" said Adam, cuttingly, and Lee cackled. Barney, as ever, was better occupied with physical entities and he left the conceptual things to us. He had found a stick and was bashing leaves from the hedge of somebody's front garden. Quick mental check: immoral? (no); illegal? (not sure); dangerous? (no – except that the owner might want to kill us if he sees); destructive? (yes! Definitely yes!).

"Barney, please stop bashing the hedge with that stick. It's damaging the hedge and we can be sure that the owner does not want his hedge damaged."

Barney banged the hedge with an almighty stroke.

"Barney! Obedience!"

Barney then hurled the stick which went flying through the air and landed in the far side of the road. As if from nowhere a car appeared and drove over the stick. The fact that the stick had missed hitting the car by only a couple of seconds left me tense. With relief I shepherded the boys off the 'yellow' road and onto a public footpath through the fields.

"Come on lads. This way."

The rain, although forecast, was still holding off. I was thankful for that, even if the overall impression of our environment was a dull and miserable battleship grey!

"How far is it?" asked Barney.

How do I answer this? Does he really want to know how far, in miles or kilometres? Or does he want to know how long it will take? Either way, the answer is likely to mean very little to him. Nevertheless, I decided to go for the distance option.

"Probably about as far as walking from our house to school 20 times," I hazarded. I know that if I give the answer to Barney in hours or minutes he will almost certainly respond by asking, "How long is that?"

∞ ∞ ∞

Perception of time

Children, and adults, with ADHD (ADDers) seem to experience time in a very different way to us ASSes. To give a detailed description of the difference is way beyond me without the assistance of a writer who himself has ADHD. Thom Hartmann(12) states that most non-ADD people describe time as a fairly consistent and linear flow. ADDers, on the other hand, have an exaggerated sense of urgency when they are involved in a task and an exaggerated sense of boredom when they feel they have nothing to do. This elastic sense of time impacts many ADDer-adults profoundly. The lows can feel as though they will last indefinitely while the highs are often perceived as flashing by. It is thought that the different way in which ADDers perceive time is due to the lower activity level in the brain at the basal ganglia areas.

With Barney, I am very aware that the only time which he truly relates to is the present – the here and now – and that both future and past exist for him in a very fuzzy, abstract way, whose mysteries cannot be easily penetrated, if at all. He certainly can and does remember past events, and can recount one or two particularly unforgettable experiences years later. For instance, when he was four years old and we were living in northern Nigeria, I threw him onto his bed one night after he had repeatedly got out of it and interrupted the adults' meal. Unfortunately I forgot to take account of mid-air acrobatics. Barney arched his back while in flight, his head position altered in relation to his centre of gravity, and the left side of his skull caught the edge of the headboard. Result? Bang! Crack! Screams! Blood (his). Tears (his and mine). Remorse (mine). An indelible memory for us all.

Even seven years later Barney would frequently remind me of this. But he could not say whether the event happened a week, a month, a year or a number of years ago. He only could remember that we were in Nigeria at the time. Similarly with future time. He never used the terms 'next week', 'next month', 'next year'. They were not part of his vocabulary even though he heard these terms frequently. The limits of his understanding of time extend from the day before yesterday until the day after tomorrow, since he readily uses the words 'yesterday-yesterday' (meaning two days ago) and 'tomorrow-tomorrow' (meaning two days hence). This relative distortion of time for the ADDer, as seen from an ASSinine perspective, has enormous implications. Unless we realise the difference in our notion of time we can all too easily misjudge the past actions or future intentions of an ADDer. We may even think that they are deliberately setting out to deceive us, when they refer to a past event in a way which sounds as if they are reporting it as happening at a different time. In other words, it is easy to think that an ADDer is also a liar.

In the 1940s an educationalist called Norwood identified a group of children who lived very much in the present tense. A child from this group, he suggested, would be suited to attend a so-called 'modern' school. He described such a pupil as one who *"deals more easily with concrete things than with ideas...(and who) is interested only in the moment (and is) essentially practical"*.[13] This is a pretty good description of our Barney, though I concede that it would also fit many children who do not have ADHD. We need educationalists who recognise these children 'interested in the moment' and who are seeking to provide suitable schools for them.

∞ ∞ ∞

"Oh fiddlesticks!" I stopped abruptly and the boys walked into one another, domino style.

"What's the matter?" asked Lee.

"We've missed our turning," I replied. "It's my fault. Too much talking and too little navigating. We should have turned off this footpath onto another one back there somewhere."

"Where?" Adam questioned my statement. "I didn't see another footpath."

"Well it's marked on the map. One problem might be that the map is old. Footpaths get changed. Never mind. If we keep going this way, we can eventually pick up a bridleway – see that red-dashed line?" I pointed to the map. "If we follow that, we can pick up the footpath again, down to that village, walk under the railway line and then over to the canal."

"Fine. Let's go." said Lee.

It soon became clear to me that the relationship between what appeared on the map and what appeared on the ground was not what it should be. I kept stopping, briefly, surveying both map and landscape.

"Are we lost?" Lee gave me his quizzical look – one which hinted at suspicion and even a little scorn.

"No – well, not really. It's all a matter of scale. I know we're here, where we are standing. That's obvious. And we're somewhere between Stiltington station and Merricott village, so in that sense we're not lost at all."

"We *are* lost!" persisted Lee, his ever-changing facial expression now having assumed the guise of a rather exasperated parent scolding his child.

"Well, we can at least take great consolation from a very important fact – one which can give us enormous encouragement at all times on this expedition." I claimed.

"And what fact is that?" asked Adam.

"The fact that I have never, ever been permanently lost yet. So you are all in good hands! Look, I'm sure if we carry on down here we'll soon come to a track leading up to Homely Farm, and we should find that bridleway just before we meet the track. Let's put our best feet forward lads. More chocolate when we get to Merricott."

"Chocolate – yes, yes, yes!" they exclaimed.

We did indeed find a track which led to a farm. But the track was more than just a track. It was a fully tarmaced driveway. A grand pair of red-brick gateposts flanked the drive, and the sign on one of the gateposts read 'Mile End Farm', not 'Homely Farm'. Added to that, there was no sign whatsoever of a bridleway on the right side of the driveway, or anywhere for that matter. I ground to a halt again. Could the farm really have changed it's name? Farms usually kept their names for years – generation after generation.

"Hang on boys!" I continued pondering the map, but was distracted from my deliberations when I realised that Lee appeared to be talking to the red bricks.

"Excuse me!" he was saying. "Can you help us please? We're explorers and we're lost."

I stared in astonishment at him. Yes, he was definitely addressing the bricks. His head was cocked upwards and his eyes appeared to be transfixed upon one particular brick. I drew nearer to him to get a better view of just what he was up to. Had he gone mad?

"Excuse me!" he repeated. "Please can you help us? We're explorers and we're lost. Is this the bridleway?"

"Lee!" I gasped, horrified, as I finally saw what was happening.

There upon the bricks was a small button and above the button was a grille. Out of this grille came static electrical-type noises and the garbled sound of a human voice. There was obviously an intercom between the farmhouse and the gateway.

"Lee, move out the way please!"

I took over where Lee had left off, caught unprepared to communicate, at such short notice, with the owner of the voice. It was a woman's voice. She sounded agitated – defensive even.

"Hello!" I began "We're just a party of walkers. We're trying to find the bridleway which should be around here somewhere according to our map....". She interrupted. I stopped speaking. So did she. I began speaking again, but so did she. We had difficulty speaking in sequence and hearing what the other was saying. I was tempted to say "Over" when I finished my sentence. Eventually our conversation assumed a comfortable rhythm and we managed to exchange words with the regularity of tennis players exchanging shots in a prolonged rally.

"Who are you? What do you want?" she demanded.

"We're just some ordinary walkers and we're a bit puzzled. We're trying to find a bridleway which crosses the land around Homely Farm but we can't see any sign of it."

"We're Homely Farm. Well, we used to be, that is. We changed our name to Mile End Farm a few years ago. Your map must be a very old one."

"Well that's good. At least we're in the right place, but we still can't find the bridleway."

"The bridleway's been diverted. It goes along the roadside now. You'll have to go that way." Her voice was brusque, dismissive, unwelcoming.

Roads were bad news when walking with Adam, Lee and Barney. I persisted.

"Would it be possible for us to take the drive up to the farmhouse and then pick up the footpath which runs into Merricott?"

"You don't want to take the footpath," she informed us.

Oh yes we do, I thought.

"But we like footpaths," I replied, as enthusiastically as possible. "In fact we love them."

"No, you won't like this footpath. The road's much better. Take the road."

"But presumably it is still a public footpath, isn't it?"

"Yes," she conceded, albeit with exasperation, "it is public, but it's unsuitable. It's very muddy at present."

"Mud's no problem to us – absolutely no problem whatsoever."

"But the road is better," she almost barked at us.

Oh no it's not, I thought, stubborn but determined to stay polite...if possible.

"OK," I said "I think we get the message. Is it that you don't want us on your land?"

This already difficult conversation was made all the more difficult by the antics of the boys. Keeping still was almost impossible for them, so they were climbing up the gateposts. I was trying desperately to sustain the dialogue and bring it to a satisfactory conclusion while simultaneously plucking boys, along with their assorted waving arms and legs, off the brickwork. My suggestion to the woman that she did not want us on her land proved to be a red rag to a bull. Her response took me aback – literally. I backed away from the intercom grille as her voice doubled in volume while seeming to rise by several octaves.

"I did not say that. I did not say that."

She sounded hysterical by now.

"Fine. That's absolutely fine," I responded, my voice rising too, despite my best efforts. "Come on kids, let's go!"

I removed my finger from the button. The boys and I looked at each other in wide-eyed silence.

"Wow!" I gasped finally, "Never mind. The road it will have to be, but we'll stop for chocolate in Merricott."

∞ ∞ ∞

Rejected and despised

Rejection is a fairly frequent experience for a child with ADHD, and his family, but it is usually after a more prolonged acquaintance than this encounter at the farm gate. Barney and Adam had both had more than their fair share of rejections, in their short lives. Every birthday, throughout his childhood, Barney would have about 11 other children to his party. I think I enjoyed these events even more than he did. We would have the usual balloons, assorted foods, jellies, ice-cream and cake, and above all plenty of wacky games. But as the years passed, the number of return invitations which Barney received to another child's party was pitifully small – one or two at the most. It was the same with invitations home to tea after school. Often our house was full of children but Barney was seldom invited back.

A candid little girl once came up to me as I waited for Barney at the school gate and said:

"Mummy says she'd like to ask Barney back to tea but she just can't cope." At least there were benevolent feelings behind that particular family's one-way relationship with us, I remember thinking. Then there was the telephone call which I received from another mother who brought it to my attention that Barney had repeatedly been using the 'F'-word in front of her own son. She made it clear that she did not want my son to associate with hers and lead him astray. This was before we understood that Barney had ADHD – before we knew what that meant, and therefore before we could even begin to explain to other people why he behaved as he did. It was before we could begin to help him to help himself. When eventually he was diagnosed with ADHD at eight years of age and was prescribed Ritalin, he became far better focussed and more able to control his actions. Gradually, very gradually, people adjusted to his more user-friendly behaviour and invitations to parties and home for tea began to be reciprocated. Barney's social life really started from here.

Adam was 11 years old when he was diagnosed with ADHD. The fact that he was also significantly dyslexic had only recently been picked up too, when he was examined by an educational psychologist. Amazingly, none of the schools which he had attended had considered this a serious problem which merited investigation. Adam's school life had deteriorated so badly by that time that his parents had had to remove him from one school and place him, at considerable cost, at another, which was more sympathetic and helpful towards boys with special educational needs. This was considered necessary to stop him suffering and resorting to self-harm because of his mounting distress. Adam's mother (Susan) and I were later interviewed by a Canadian woman who was doing a PhD on ADHD. She had a teenager with ADHD – a girl. During the interview she painfully described how, once her daughter became mobile, she found that she didn't belong to the 'Mummy Club' any more. She asked whether we had had similar experiences and we both answered 'Yes'. Many people had withdrawn from us, as if protecting their children, and themselves, from our sons, and even from us, as though contamination might occur through association.

∞ ∞ ∞

Rejection, yes. We had survived it before and we would survive it again. Ploughing our way through mud and long grass on the narrowing verge we set off for Merricott.

Chapter 10

Metanoia...(Repentance)

"Metanoia" (μετανοια) *Greek Noun = Repentance. A turning about.*

A complete change of direction.

We had been walking along the verge for no more than two minutes when an extraordinary thing happened. A car approached us and slowed down, and, as I glanced over my left shoulder, I saw an extremely classy BMW with a woman driver. The car drew to a halt alongside us. Instinctively I knew who she was.

"Hello!" she called. "I'm from Mile End Farm. We were talking just now!". She had to shout.

I turned to the boys who had stopped in their tracks.

"Now listen very carefully. I'm going to talk to the lady and all three of you MUST stay here. We're on a very nasty bend and you can't see what's coming round the corner. Under no circumstances whatsoever will you follow me. Barney, do you understand?"

"Yes."

"Adam, do you understand?"

"Yes."

"Lee, do you understand?"

"Yes."

"Good! So please stay here and wait for me."

They stared at the car and it's occupant. I gingerly crossed the road. Smiling as I approached, I decided that the best policy, as usual, was transparent openness – an explanation of who we were, what we were doing, and why it was desirable, if not actually necessary, to go about it in our particular way.

"Hello," she said again – a far more composed woman than the one we had left squawking down the intercom. "My name's Jenny – Jenny Newbold. I thought I'd just come and see if you were OK."

Mrs Newbold was very spruce, smartly dressed, well made-up and a very handsome woman approaching middle-age. She glanced sheepishly, and with interest, at the boys on the other side of the road and quickly added:

"We've had a bit of trouble in the past with vandals and with young people messing about with the intercom. My teenage son answered your buzzing. He didn't know what to make of it and passed you over to me."

I remembered Lee's unorthodox introduction and wasn't surprised that a young lad on the receiving end had taken fright.

"I can see now," she added "that you're not those sort of people at all. But you know the footpath to Merricott is very muddy – very muddy indeed."

"I'd better explain my insistence." It was my turn to talk, and even though I was standing in the middle of the road, it was far easier to communicate now than it had been through the grille. Body language and facial expression add so much to our understanding of the intention behind someone's words. "My name's Anna, and two of those three boys over there suffer from Attention Deficit Hyperactivity Disorder. One of them, Barney, is my son. The others are his friends. Have you heard of Attention Deficit Hyperactivity Disorder – ADHD?"

"Er, yes. I think so. I'm not quite sure."

"Well, in a nutshell, it means that they have masses and masses of energy which has to be dissipated safely. Taking them on long country walks is an excellent way to do this, which is why we are out and about. Having ADHD makes it very difficult for them to concentrate and pay attention so they are very likely to wander, or more likely lurch, out into the middle of the road. There's a great danger of them getting run over if we have to walk along a winding road without a pavement."

I pointed to where the Merricott Lane curved sharply to the right, a visual aid for the point I was making. She looked appropriately horrified, yet understanding and sympathetic.

"So you see," I continued, "that's why I'm trying to guide us along as many footpaths and bridleways as possible, and avoid all roads. Compared with a road, mud is far more desirable. Mud is fun. It might make us dirty, but it won't kill us. A car could."

"Yes I see. But where are you going to after Merricott?"

I drew breath. "Tappenham Youth Hostel."

"But you're going in completely the opposite direction!"

"I know. We're taking the scenic route."

"Oh!" She was now completely nonplussed.

Then came a totally unexpected change in her attitude.

"Would you like to bring the boys back to the farmhouse? You could have a cup of tea and I'll give the boys some drinks and biscuits."

Wow! I had to think very quickly. I still felt slightly on edge and exposed, standing in the middle of the road. The boys' patience could run out at any time. I had to re-assess the whole situation and try to think through the likely consequences of a change of plan. I couldn't do it that quickly, but I did manage to convince myself that a change of plan in the middle of lowland, temperate England was unlikely to become dangerous or life-threatening. Go for it! I thought.

In my experience, the unexpected was to be welcomed with open arms. There were risks, true, but they were usually risks that were worth taking. The unexpected was also exciting, and the experience is often life-enriching and the precursor of other adventures.

"That would be fantastic. That's really, really kind of you. We'd love to come. I know the boys will be really pleased."

"They can have a game of snooker. Do they like snooker? We have a full-size table."

"Do they like snooker? They absolutely love snooker. Barney is crazy about it."

"Well that's settled then. I'll drive back and I'll see you and the boys at the farmhouse in a few minutes."

She pressed a button somewhere within the depths of the car and the window closed. I crossed the road back to the boys while Jenny Newbold drove on a short way towards Merricott so that she could turn the car around.

"Boys!" I said excitedly, "we're off on another adventure! We've been invited back to the farmhouse by Mrs Newbold, the lady who lives there. It must be a mansion house because they are very rich and they have a snooker table. You're to be treated like kings! You shall eat biscuits and sip drinks of your choice. You shall be ushered to a full-size snooker table and play snooker to your hearts' content." I fed their imaginations unashamedly as much as possible, eager to 'milk' this amazing opportunity for all it was worth, and no doubt overdoing it in the process.

The boys looked at me with incredulity.

"Are we going to stay there?" asked Lee.

"Oh no. We're not going to stay there overnight. We'll only stay there a little while – as long as it takes to have some drinks and a biscuit – and a game of snooker, of course."

"But why has she asked us?" said Adam.

"A good question. I think she was sorry for giving us the impression that she was turning us away from her land. Then as soon as she actually saw you, she realised what brilliant young men you are and thought how honoured she would be if you were to grace her house with your presence."

"Oh yeah." Lee's sarcasm was cutting. His wide eyes and infinitely flexible face signalled a host of unspoken words, like "Pull the other one" or, "You've got to be joking".

Adam stared blankly at me. Barney was silent but glanced rapidly from one to the other, trying to unravel this puzzling turn of events and grasp what was actually happening and why.

"Well come on lads!" I said as I set off back the way we came. "We're not going to look a gift horse in the mouth!"

"We're going to a rich lady's house," mused Adam.

"Did you see that car?" interjected Lee. "And that driveway looked very smart too."

The evidence was plain for all to see. She was certainly rich. But why had she pursued us, and then offered us such gracious hospitality? I pondered the matter, trying to see events from her perspective.

As we entered the driveway between the gateposts, Adam said:

"Can I press the button and tell her we're coming?"

"No. That won't be necessary Adam, thank you. She knows we're on our way."

"Why didn't she give us a lift in her car?" asked Lee.

I had been wondering that myself.

It took us several minutes to walk along the driveway, during which time I imagined the scene. Mrs Newbold would be scurrying around the 'palace', hurriedly briefing the rest of her family before our arrival, sweeping up the silverware in her path and concealing it in a brown canvas holdall. Piles of dirty washing would be removed and placed, maybe, into a gigantic farm-sized washing machine. The Rottweiler would be hastily unchained from his kennel and he would be trotting now, tail wagging, towards the farmhouse wondering why, all of a sudden, it was his lucky day.

Before we reached the farmhouse, we came to a large barn. The barn door was open and beside a modern four-wheel drive vehicle stood a green-wellied man and woman. They wore Barbour jackets. They saw us at about the same time we saw them and, without a word, they stared at us. But their demeanour was by no means hostile and they almost managed a smile.

"Hello"! I greeted them cheerily, "We've just met the lady of the house and she's invited us back for tea."

"Jenny did?" gasped the man.

"Yes, it is rather surprising, isn't it?" I beamed at him.

The woman at his side poked him in the ribs, hard.

"He didn't mean it like that," she eagerly tried to cover for him.

I disagreed. "I think he probably did, but we don't mind. After all, I'd be thinking the same thing in his position".

They grinned sheepishly and pointed us in the direction of the farmhouse – a modern, impeccably built and maintained home welcomed us. We yanked off our boots, removed our rucksacks and left them all under the overhanging eaves. The door was open.

Chapter 11

Guests of Honour

"The rich man in his castle,
The poor man at his gate,
He made them high and lowly
And ordered their estate."

(From 'All Things Bright and Beautiful' – pre-expurgation – by Mrs C F Alexander)

"Come on in." Jenny Newbold was waiting for us at the door.

I was warming to her more and more. How kind it was of her not only to swallow her pride, but also to make us so welcome. How rare that we should experience such acceptance and selfless hospitality.

The light and modern house was spotlessly clean, surprising for a farmhouse, I thought. The entrance hall was roomy, the painted walls adorned with pictures and photographs, and the floor laid with sparkling tiles which extended into the kitchen through a door on the right. If the hall was spacious, the kitchen was even more so. In addition to the usual fitted section, it extended into a dining area complete with a large table and chairs. Beyond that were armchairs and a sofa and a thick warm rug decked the floor. A pair of large glass patio doors led to a small green patch of lawn.

There was no Rottweiler, but as we were ushered through, a sleek black cat sidled nonchalantly up to Lee, completely unperturbed by our entry. Lee was immediately enchanted by the beast.

"Oh, what a lovely cat. He's absolutely gorgeous...or is 'he' a 'she'?"

"A 'she' actually," said Jenny "well, er that is to say she was a she..."

"You mean she's a 'he' now?" Lee queried.

"No, No. She used to be a 'she', but well, then she had an operation and..."

"Oh I get it!" interjected Lee, again, "She's a trans-, trans-, trans- what's the word?"

I started laughing. Poor Jenny blushed as she tried to interrupt Lee before he finished the offensive word. The cat was not the only one pussy-footing around!

"Oh no, no! Not one of those! She's had an operation and it means she can't have kittens. She's been neutered."

"Oh, right. I see." said Lee, and Jenny looked relieved. All the boys were fussing over the cat by now.

"What would you like to drink boys? We've got fruit juices, Ribena or lemonade."

Barney, Adam and Lee made their selection. Jenny put the kettle on for our tea and then opened the biscuit tin. The tin of home-made cookies was passed around.

A teenage boy entered the kitchen.

"Roger! Come and meet Anna, Barney, Adam and Lee." Jenny's hand gesticulated to each of us in turn as we were introduced. "It was Roger who spoke to you first over the intercom."

"It was Lee who pressed the button."

We laughed. Roger, evidently, was rather shy.

"Have you got any other children?" asked Adam, not in the least bit shy.

"Yes, a daughter, Annabel."

"A daughter?" Lee's eyes opened wide with interest.

Jenny chuckled, mildly surprised in so great an interest from such a young boy.

"Well, she's a bit too old for you, young man!"

"How old is she?" persisted Lee.

"Sixteen."

"Sixteen? Oh, lovely!" said Lee, his eyes now gleaming with anticipation.

"I must apologise for him. Age appears to present no problem to Lee. I'm embarrassed to say that on the first train which we took today, Lee 'chatted up' a 17 year old girl."

Jenny was genuinely astonished. All eyes were on Lee now.

"But wasn't she surprised when she found out your age, if she did find it out, that is?" she asked, addressing Lee directly.

"Oh, I just told her I was 17 too."

"I don't think she will have believed that," said Jenny, gently.

"I told her that I had a growth problem!" He meant it, too.

You had to hand it to Lee. He was supremely entertaining. Jenny shook her head in amused disbelief.

"Roger!" she called. "Please take the boys to the snooker room. I'm sure they'd all love a game."

Up went a cheer from the three youngsters. The teenager obeyed, silently.

Jenny made the tea and we both sat down at the big pine table.

"Tell me again what condition your son has," she said.

"ADHD. It stands for Attention Deficit Hyperactivity Disorder."

"Has he had it a long time?"

"Yes," I smiled, "almost certainly since birth. In fact most probably since he was conceived. Barney is adopted. It is very likely that one, or even both of his birth-parents also had the condition, because it's often inherited."

"So did you know he had it when you adopted him?"

"No, not at all. We didn't have a clue. We collected Barney straight from hospital when he was 27 days old. He'd been born very prematurely – about seven or eight weeks early. He only weighed four pounds at birth. The hospital wanted to fatten him up before releasing him to us and, I think, check him over thoroughly and keep an eye on his early development. I think they felt particularly obliged to do as thorough a job as possible because Barney was being placed for adoption, and they felt it important that the prospective new parents should have as much information about the baby as possible."

"So did everything seem normal then?"

"More or less. He was still very small when we went to collect him – about six pounds. His breathing was rapid and very noisy. He made a clicking sound in his throat with every breath. We were told it was just that his respiratory system was immature, and that it would cease with time. It did. Also, just before he was released to us, a paediatrician picked up a heart murmur during the final checks. Barney was taken immediately to a hospital in London to have his heart scanned. The apparatus which they used was so new that the doctors were, apparently, struggling to interpret what they saw, but they reckoned there was nothing very much wrong with his heart."

"Well, he certainly appears lively enough! When did you find out about his ADHD?"

"Well, I could answer that by saying 'as soon as he became mobile', but in another sense the answer would be when he was about eight years old."

"When did he become mobile?"

"Around the normal time I'd say, but maybe he was a little bit delayed because of his prematurity. He started walking at 16 months, and once he started he didn't stop. He headed straight for the horizon!"

"That must have been difficult to cope with?"

"Well, it wasn't just the walking. It was his overall, relentless activity. He wouldn't accept being restrained without an almighty battle. Take his buggy, for instance. It came supplied with the usual over-the-shoulder and between-the-legs harnesses and clips. But Barney would wriggle free and escape. So we had to dress him in an additional harness, and clip that to the rings at the side of the buggy. When he went in the back-pack he had to be clipped in, and I remember him climbing out nonetheless, and dangling from the frame on my back. It was dangerous, uncomfortable and exasperating because there was no way we could use that back-pack."

"I wonder why he would want to climb out. He must've had a good view from up there?"

"A good question. I've long since come to the conclusion that what might seem sensible and desirable to you and me is by no means either sensible or desirable for Barney. There must be other factors which seem more desirable than enjoying a good view, or some kind of compulsion which forces him to try and escape."

"It must've been a nightmare trying to get him to stay in bed," Jenny added thoughtfully.

"In bed? It was a nightmare trying to keep him inside his cot, and it was years before we could even consider moving him into a bed! We soon learned that if we had the patience to scoop him up 99 times after he had clambered out of his cot and tobogganed down the stairs in his sleep-suit, Barney had the persistence to do it 100 times. He would just keep on doing it, apparently tirelessly, and he showed very little frustration, while we were seething and almost going out of our minds! In the end, we made a lid out of a large sheet of chipboard."

"Goodness me! What did he think of that?"

"Not a lot. He pushed the lid off. So we had to tie it on. We were relieved that Barney had been officially adopted by then because once the adoption was final the visits from social workers stopped. If they'd done one of their surprise visits and found our son incarcerated, then Aaron and I would have been the ones to have ended up behind bars. But what else could we do? It might appear to be cruel at first sight, but we were sure that he needed to sleep – doesn't everybody? We certainly did! And as for locking a child in, well, all parents do that when they lock and bolt the house up at night. It's just a matter of scale, really. The principle's the same." Or so I tried to justify our actions.

Jenny looked thoughtful. "Don't some children get hyperactive when they eat particular things, especially if they have those really bright food colourings?" she questioned.

"Yes, some children do." I agreed. "Some children go crazy. Tartrazine, a synthetic yellow dye, was one of the earliest known culprits, but I don't think it can be legally added to foodstuffs or soft drinks any more. I knew one boy, who's grown up now, who became uncontrollably hyperactive when he ate eggs with bright yellow, or possibly orange, yolks. His mother discovered that he could safely eat eggs from her friend's hens who hadn't been fed with the dye which makes the yolks so gloriously technicoloured."

"So have you tried adjusting Barney's diet at all? Could that help, do you think?"

"Up to a point," I replied, "but we've always been very careful about food colourings and additives. When Barney was two years old and his amazing activity levels became obvious, it seemed to coincide with a sudden increase in public awareness of a possible connection between foodstuffs and hyperactivity. I certainly remember paying a lot of attention to the matter at the time. I was very careful about what he ate. We kept a copy of the book which listed all the additives. I learned off by heart the 'E' numbers, chemical names and side-effects of many compounds and spent hours gazing at the small-print on food labels."

"And did you reach any conclusion?"

"Yes, I did, eventually. Quite a firm one as it happens. And it all came about because of the amount of travelling we did between 1990 and 1992."

"Travelling? What do you mean?"

"Well, in 1990, when Barney was two, we took him to Tanzania (where my husband was working temporarily), to Poland (where my relatives live) and to Greece (for a holiday). We also spent a lot of time in England. The thing that struck me was that whatever we fed Barney, whatever the climate was like or whether we were north or south of the equator, he was always the same. By that I mean he was always active: always straining at the harness; always running off towards the horizon if unrestrained. Barney's diet was substantially different in Tanzania, Poland, Greece and England, but his behaviour seemed consistently hyperactive and quite unaffected by the changes. Then in 1992, when he was four, we spent three months living in northern Nigeria. We were based in a small town and the vast majority of our food came from the local market. We ate unprocessed food, grown and reared locally, which was, to the best of our knowledge, produced without the addition of pesticides or artificial fertilizers."

"And what was Barney's activity level like then?"

"The same as ever. *Super-ballistic*, as one friend used to describe him!"

"So does that mean that hyperactivity isn't affected by foodstuffs?"

"Not in Barney's case. As far as I know there is little scientific evidence to support dietary manipulation as being a worthwhile treatment for kids with ADHD. You see, even though some children do become less hyperactive if a particular substance is eliminated from their diet, it does nothing to tackle their impulsiveness and poor concentration, which are the main core symptoms of ADHD."[14]

"I still can't help thinking that food just might be involved somehow," Jenny mused, "I mean so many medical conditions do seem to be either caused by certain foods or at the very least exacerbated by them."

"That's true." I had to admit that Jenny had a very good point. "Maybe someone, sometime, will find out that people with ADHD have a genetic predisposition for their neurology to be altered by some commonly-occurring substance in food. I remember reading that some scientists think nutrition, in particular wheat and milk intake, is of great importance in schizophrenia, and that's a condition which is linked with brain chemistry like ADHD. I have heard of isolated instances of children with ADHD whose parents claim that they've improved when taking a fish-oil supplement."

"Why not try that with Barney then?"

"We did, a few years ago. We bought some fish oil capsules and fed them to Barney daily for some months. But we couldn't detect any difference and they were very expensive. We stopped giving them to him in the end. Overall, I feel that I've done what is reasonable in the food-investigation line, and we have to give Barney something to eat. We obviously can't let him starve. So we go on trying to give him as balanced a diet as we can, while being vigilant about additives. In the meantime, we just have to accept that, like it or not, life with Barney resembles an action movie running at top speed!"

Jenny was getting the picture of what living with an ADHD child can be like.

"Raising Barney must have been exhausting."

"It was. He was. He still is, actually."

"You are brave, bringing him away like this, and the other boys, too."

"Well, if the truth be told, not only am I really fond of Adam and Lee too, and enjoy their company, but also I actually find it easier to take the three of them away than just Barney on his own."

Jenny was surprised. "But didn't you say that Adam has ADHD too?"

"Yes, he has. He only had it formally diagnosed a couple of weeks ago. But the thing with Barney is that he's so much easier to live with when he's diluted with other children. He gets distracted by them you see – for good or ill, but for the most-part it's good. He takes his lead from them. It's as if he doesn't really know what to do by himself. He finds it difficult to organise himself even in the act of playing, but if he has other children around, he watches what they do and simply copies them. Other children are his visual aids. He finds it extremely hard to follow spoken instructions in any setting, or to conjure up a mental image of what he should be doing and then execute the task."

"But, well, how can I put it... he looks so normal."

"Yes, that's the twist, and it's a cruel twist a lot of the time. Because he looks so normal everyone expects him to behave and respond like the majority of children do. When he refuses to comply or simply fails at some kind of task – which is a lot of the time – he comes across as a disobedient little boy who deserves a good spanking, and 'that'll teach him!'. It doesn't...we tried that. When he was young, and even now really, he simply didn't and doesn't seem to learn from punishment. He fails time and again to find a link between cause and effect. It was bizarre, looking back. We would ask him why he had done a certain thing and he simply couldn't say why. He didn't know. He'd forgotten. But we didn't realise that he might have short-term memory problems. We were determined that he shouldn't run wild, and like his older sister he would be a well-disciplined child. We genuinely thought he would link what we perceived as his bad behaviour with an unpleasantly stinging bottom, and refrain from doing whatever it was. But it didn't work with Barney. He cried, briefly, but went on re-offending. We had to stop the physical punishment then. Any more and our so-called disciplining would have verged on child abuse."

Jenny gave a wry smile. "You know, I'm really interested in what you're saying. You see, I'm very involved with our local branch of the NSPCC – The National Society for the Prevention of Cruelty to Children."

Chapter 12

A Question of Human Rights

"No-one should hurt you in any way. Adults should make sure that you are protected from abuse, violence and neglect. Even your parents have no right to hurt you."

"Even if you do something wrong, no-one is allowed to punish you in a way that humiliates you or hurts you badly."

(Articles 19 and 37 from the **United Nations Convention on the Rights of the Child**, 1989, Ratified by the United Kingdom of Great Britain and Northern Ireland on 16th December 1991.)

My mug hit the table with a noticeable thud and my face froze. "Oh my goodness!" I thought, "Here I am sitting down to tea, blithely revealing all about how I caged my son when he was an infant, how I've spanked him until he cried, and the very woman I'm talking to is a member of the NSPCC."

Jenny chortled gently at my expression.

"I think Barney's doing very well, all things considered," she said graciously and added "I can see that he's very lively but he must be behaving OK in the snooker room or Roger would be back here like a shot. Is he growing out of his ADHD?"

I laughed softly. "No, I don't think so. I once heard a neurologist ask, rhetorically, 'Does a person grow out of his brain?' Unfortunately, Jenny, almost all children who have ADHD will grow up to become adults with ADHD. Very occasionally you get the odd one or two who lose their symptoms when they grow up, but it's rare. You see, the thing which determines Barney's ADHD is his brain and the way it works. I really hesitate to say that his brain isn't normal and that it's therefore abnormal. I think it's better and truer to say that his brain is simply different. There's nothing to be ashamed of in anyone having a different sort of brain, and I really think the fact that it's still sometimes treated as shameful is totally unnecessary and unhelpful. We don't need to attach any stigma to it. Aaron and I don't. We refuse to. An ADHD-type brain is different to my brain, and to yours too, I think, and the difference is a relative under-functioning of the frontal lobes," I said, gently tapping my skull in the region of my forehead. "Barney is on some medication, Ritalin, which stimulates the frontal lobes of his brain and helps him to concentrate better. When he can concentrate better, he can also control himself better. He becomes less hyperactive as his mind focuses, and he's better able to make and execute choices. Then he can carry out tasks more easily. Because he does want to please other people most of the time, it has the overall effect of making him appear outwardly more obedient."

"Only outwardly?"

"Well, from a moral stand-point, I sometimes wonder if it makes a real difference. After all, he could have been wanting to please me, or his school teacher say, when in a similar situation while unmedicated, but he would have failed miserably through no real fault of his own. But it's great when he is obedient. Not only does it make life easier for everyone, but Barney experiences success, congratulations and positive feedback. He gets a buzz, and his self-esteem goes up for a change."

"I should think that a child with ADHD could end up with very poor self-esteem," Jenny pondered.

"Absolutely! In fact, you've hit the nail on the head. Take Adam for example. His ADHD has been undiagnosed all his life, and the formal diagnosis by a paediatrician only came this month. I'm afraid that his teachers didn't understand Adam at all, and saw his failures as deliberate acts of obstreperousness. They kept on punishing him and then excluded him from school lunches for some trivial offence which was totally misinterpreted, and he was never given the chance to explain his side of the story."

"What on earth had he done?"

"He'd tipped un-drunk water from the beakers at the school dinner table back into the jug, which was against the rules. I suppose it was a matter of hygiene. Fair enough. But what the school never discovered was that Adam's reason for his actions had been to try and save water! He'd honestly been trying to help! His self-esteem became so low that he even started to injure himself. The punishments and exclusion were so hurtful to both Adam and his family that his parents felt they had no option but to remove him from the school."

"That's absolutely wicked!" Jenny was genuinely appalled. Her natural sensitivity to the mistreatment of children came shining through.

"Well, it would have been wicked if the teachers knew what they were doing. But if they were merely unaware, then it would simply be a mistake. A 'school' as an authority is really a combination of many teachers plus the head, and each of them may have had different levels of understanding about Adam's condition, and their own individual motives for acting in the way they did."

"Yes, that's true. People can really only treat children with ADHD properly if they know about the condition, and understand it. I'm meeting up with our local NSPCC group in a few days time."

Jenny looked as though she was wondering just how she could raise awareness among her colleagues. This, I thought, was an opportunity not to be missed!

"Would you like me to send you some literature about ADHD which you could distribute among your friends?"

"Oh, could you? That would be marvellous!"

It was settled. We exchanged addresses so that I could post the information on.

"You know," Jenny said, shaking her head, "these children – the ones who go undiagnosed – must have a terrible time at school."

"Some, if not most, of them do," I agreed. "Between the ages of five and 16 the law forces them to be educated, and for the vast majority of children with ADHD this means daily discomfort or torture in a place called school. And it gets worse and worse the older they get, as their frustrations increase and their failures mount up. They're trapped. It's a kind of slavery really - a form of abuse. I'm sure that kind of schooling being imposed on them is a violation of their human rights. Take that idea to your NSPCC group!"

Jenny sat with her elbow on the table and her chin cupped in her hand. "Have you ever contacted the NSPCC about any of this?" she asked.

"Yes, as a matter of fact I have, just two weeks ago. I sent them a very thorough letter explaining the situation as best I could. It tied in very well with their 'Cruelty to Children Must Stop; Full Stop' campaign which they've recently launched. I'm sure you know all about it."

"Yes, quite a lot! Our next committee meeting is going to be dealing with that as the main agenda item."

"What the NSPCC decides to do about cruelty to children with ADHD remains to be seen, Jenny. It depends partly on whether they believe me or not. And even if they do, it depends on whether they have the desire to tackle such a complex and hidden form of cruelty. It's easy to step in when an abused child has cuts and bruises, but how do you justify intervention when the cruelty is invisible and locked into an inappropriate education system? It will take a very convinced, very courageous person to do that," I said.

"Yes, I suppose it will."

∞ ∞ ∞

"I'll put the kettle on for another cup of tea."

Jenny rose from the table and as she was filling the kettle she said, "I think I'll just go and check up on the boys and see that they're OK".

"How kind of her to be so concerned for the well-being of Barney, Adam and Lee", I thought. Only some considerable time later did it cross my mind that her overriding concern had almost certainly been to see whether Roger was coping and whether her furniture, walls and carpets were surviving the onslaught of my three lads!

Jenny soon returned to the kitchen.

"They're fine," she said as she made the tea, then launching straight back into our earlier conversation, she continued. "Tell me; have you ever thought about educating Barney at home?"[15]

"Yes I have," I said with feeling.

"And?"

"And I've rejected the possibility, if one could even call it a possibility."

"Well, why not? Why don't you think it's possible or practical?"

"How long have you got?" I smiled, and continued. "Firstly, Barney would be on his own and have no peers to follow. He depends so much on being able to follow the crowd. The other kids are his visual aids. They indicate to him, without knowing, what he's meant to be doing, even something as simple to you or me as sitting on a chair. Secondly, a home-educated child who has only one tutor (me, for instance) is totally at the mercy of the health and well-being of that tutor, in addition to his own ailments and afflictions. My own health is erratic so I could never provide Barney with the kind of continuity in his education which he needs. Thirdly, there are subjects like PE which are no fun all by yourself. As for getting Barney to play games or do athletics, unaccompanied, in a meaningful and organised manner, well, it's rather like trying to get a greyhound to run around a racetrack with no hare to chase."

Jenny nodded her head and laughed. I smiled back and continued.

"Fourthly, if Barney and I were alone together in a teaching situation, we'd have driven one another completely mad by the end of the day. And fifthly, Barney wouldn't learn how to interact socially."

"OK, I can see the impracticalities of it now. It must take a very particular kind of child and parent who, together, can make it work. Though I suppose there is no reason why the tutor has to be the child's parent."

"That's true," I agreed "but even if the tutor were someone from outside the family and supplied by the Local Education Authority, most of my points would still apply."

We thought about this in silence for a few seconds and I finished my tea. I realised that there was still so much to say and not enough time to say it. I began to compose a letter in my mind…

Chapter 13

A National Neurology? (Letter to Jenny)

"The National Curriculum is all very well, but I think that a National Curriculum will not be appropriate unless and until there exists a National Neurology."

(The author)

Tuesday 2nd November 1999

Dear Jenny

Thank you so very much yet again for your amazing hospitality towards the boys and myself last Saturday. I don't think we have ever been made to feel so welcome and the boys thoroughly enjoyed their 'snooker and snacks' interval.

Well, we survived our journey, further extraordinary adventures notwithstanding! I really enjoyed our discussion, though in retrospect I'm sure that I did most of the talking. Sorry for hogging the conversation and thanks for being such a willing listener. It would have been great if we could've spent longer together because there were so many more things which I wanted to explain. I realised afterwards that I went on and on about Adam's poor self-esteem and said hardly anything about Barney's - and he's my son! I hope you don't mind me putting headings in this letter. I find it so much easier to think straight when I work to some kind of structure, so here goes!

Self-esteem, and Barney's in particular

You were so very right, Jenny, when you commented that a child with ADHD could end up with very poor self-esteem. Low self-esteem is one of the worst consequences of undiagnosed, untreated ADHD. Not long ago one of Barney's teachers contacted me because he was quite shocked and worried about Barney's low rating of self-worth. Apparently the class had been asked to identify things about themselves which were good and Barney had not been able to think of one. He listed all the people who he thought considered him to be stupid. It included us (his parents), his grandmother and his teachers. I was aghast! Until then I really thought that Aaron and I had been succeeding in showing Barney how wonderful we think he is. Remember, I am talking about a child who has been diagnosed and is being treated. Just think how much worse it must be for those kids who haven't and aren't. And the place where their self-esteem is damaged most is in school.

When they're young it's not too bad, especially if they get a good, firm teacher. Primary schools keep the children in a well-structured environment which is of great help to a kid with ADHD. For most of the school day he has one classroom in which he works, one place where he is expected to sit, one teacher who gets to know him very well indeed and will soon discover the best way to deal with him. What a shock secondary or middle school can bring. This is where it all started to crumble for Barney. What a child like Barney finds is that the frequent classroom changes are confusing, particularly as he never seems to know what the time is. No one teacher gets to know him particularly well and, I suspect, neither does any one teacher take on the responsibility for his problems because so many teachers have a share in his education. Routines are more difficult to establish and more frequently broken, and on top of it all the poor child is expected to organise his books and get the right equipment to each lesson, on time. And that's not all. He must take down instructions about homework correctly, manage to take the right books and equipment home each night, and then actually complete the homework, bring it back and hand it in. Each one of these steps is a nightmare for such a child, and all their mistakes are cruelly exposed to the view of teachers, peers and parents. Some kids I know carry all their books around all the time so that they're never without the right book. This is a tremendous physical and psychological strain for them. Others, like Barney, rarely have the right thing in the right place at the right time. No wonder the self-esteem of these children takes an awful knock. Even if they do eventually have all the right bits and pieces for the lesson, what they achieve during lessons is often minimal and very untidy. Before Barney had a one-to-one Learning Support Assistant, (LSA) he had a habit of destroying much of his work, putting it in the bin and starting, or pretending to start, all over again. He was forever breaking his pencil and spending as much time as possible sharpening it. It was all about avoidance and delay tactics!

Treating ADHD - medication, coaches and behavioural strategies

ADHD can't be cured, only treated, so that its damaging effects are minimised. Giving medication to a child (or an adult) with ADHD can help them enormously. It's true that some people with ADHD find they derive no benefit from treatment with a stimulant drug like Ritalin, though over 70 per cent of them find that it does help. If it does help, then you've still got to get the dose right. It's quite an art really. We're still trying to find the best regime for Barney. There are some people who prefer to avoid medication altogether and find that they can manage OK in life if they implement various behavioural strategies. They may find that by leading their lives in a very structured way they can cope. Adults who have ADHD and are of above average intelligence often do manage to work out their own coping-strategies. Nevertheless, sometimes 'ADDers' (as they are called) of any age or intelligence level, need help from another person - from an adult without ADHD - who checks up on them in the nicest possible way! In the case of an adult with ADHD, their helper is called a 'coach'. In the case of a child, the helper is usually a parent. As far as I can tell now it is likely that Barney will need a coach when he's an adult. The coach won't be there to criticise or nag him, but rather to support planning in his life and help him to get things done.

Some people think that coaching is the same as therapy or counselling, but it isn't. Counselling and therapy look back into the past, but coaching is more like mentoring. The past is accepted - it can't be changed, after all - and the idea is to move forward in a positive way. A coach will be able to offer better techniques and practices to Barney and help him eliminate the negative effects of living with his feelings of under-achievement. A coach can provide the necessary cues at appropriate times. Coaching is done by mutual agreement, which works toward positive changes like improvements in attitude, decision-making, prioritising and sequencing tasks, developing new skills and renewed self-confidence.[16]

Some people think it's always possible to help a kid if he or she is put through some kind of special behavioural programme and kept off medication altogether. I saw a programme on TV where a very difficult boy had his behaviour transformed by some specialised social workers. They went through a very firm but fair routine with him until he learned how to control himself and obey. His parents were taught how to use this regime too. There was no physical punishment or drugs involved at all and it certainly left me wondering whether we could do the same with Barney. But I know really that our experience has shown that this will not be successful for Barney. We read all the best books on child-rearing and tried all sorts of methods - stick, carrot, sanctions, rewards, praise wherever possible, smacking and non-punitive techniques. Barney never seemed to learn, whatever we tried, and it was heartbreaking. The best thing that happened to help him to help himself was when he went on Ritalin, shortly after his eighth birthday. As for the boy on that TV programme, I wonder whether he really had ADHD in the first place; he probably had a condition which mimics it. It was shown that the boy could regulate his own behaviour, even though it took extraordinarily labour-intensive parenting to get him to do so. That's not really the situation with the child who genuinely does have ADHD.

There have been quite a lot of studies here and in America to try and discover whether behavioural treatments work better or worse than medication, or whether a combination of both is best. In all these studies, using large samples of children or adolescents with ADHD, results consistently show that carefully worked out medication management is always superior to behavioural treatments alone. Combined medication and behavioural treatments are only modestly better than well-managed medication alone.[17] So it seems that Ritalin really does help kids to modify their own behaviour in a very positive way. We've definitely seen it with Barney. And if he can get his behaviour to improve, he gets praised by us and by his teachers, so up goes his self-esteem. Not that his self-esteem is high, far from it, but I dread to think what it would be like if he didn't have the benefit of his medication. And it's in the classroom, in particular, where medication can have such a vital part to play.

A school environment, even when the curriculum is ADHD-user-friendly, isn't an easy environment for kids like Barney. There's no point denying it - Ritalin in most cases does make it easier for a child to concentrate and conform to behaviour patterns which are vital for the smooth running of a school. To successfully educate a really hyperactive un-medicated child, I think one would have to use some kind of extremely radical alternative. I have heard that the outdoor schools of Australian aborigines are working well. I expect the kids there really get to 'interact with their curriculum'. Did I tell you that Barney has this brilliant educational psychologist called Sean? Well Sean's always talking about the need for children with ADHD to 'interact with their curriculum'.

The need for strength-centred education

Sean gives an example of 'interacting with the curriculum' which is the use of drama, dance and rap. He knows of one school which uses rap and dance to help the kids learn their multiplication tables. These are 'kinaesthetic' methods. The pupils can sense the muscular effort that they make and relate it to what they hear and what they have to memorise. It seems to work really well.

In contrast, teachers using traditional teaching methods tend to see kids with undiagnosed ADHD as naughty, unco-operative, under-achieving and defiant, not realising that they are imposing upon them an entire educational system in which the curriculum and methods centre on the children's weaknesses and not on their strengths. Sean thinks that all teachers ought to try the following thought experiment: they should try to imagine the child having to cope day-by-day at school with demands and activities based on his weaknesses. Then they should think about what they know to be their own greatest professional weakness. If they don't know, they can always ask a colleague. Next, they should imagine a school inspector repeatedly visiting them while they were carrying out duties based on their weakness, and the effect it would have on their self-esteem. And finally, they can try to identify their greatest strength, which will probably be the part of their work which gives them greatest pleasure. They should imagine the school inspector repeatedly visiting them now, while they were engaged in tasks based on this strength. What would their self-esteem be like now? I think this experiment is brilliant. It helps us all to understand the plight of ADHD children. How much better it would be if they could have an education based on their strengths.

Almost all parents of ADHD kids find themselves trying to find answers to questions such as 'Does such education exist?' and 'Do such schools exist?'. Well, I haven't found one yet in the mainstream state system. I'm aware of one school in the country which specifically, and with dedication, caters for kids with ADHD. I recently visited it with Barney. It's based on similar schools in America. We saw children studying in classrooms with fans whirring away - apparently this deadens background sounds which are so distracting to these children. Some of the kids had partitions between their desks, making them into carrels I suppose, cutting down visual distractions. As many lessons as possible for each pupil were held in their main classroom to avoid disruptive changes. There were so many practical alterations just like this to accommodate the children's difficulties. But the school is in South London and too far away for Barney to get there and back each day, even if we could afford the fares and the fees.

We also visited a school in Hampshire. It's another independent school, but unlike the London one, it does take boarders. About 90 per cent of the pupils are dyslexic - with or without ADHD. The great thing about this school is the strength-centred education which it offers. For instance, it has a motor workshop where many of the kids, especially the boys, have a great time. They really enjoy taking cars apart and putting them back together, and become more motivated in subjects like maths and physics as a result. They can see the relevance of these more difficult academic subjects to the practical activity which delights them so much. If only school could be like that for Barney and Adam - and all other children with ADHD. But it's a matter of cost again. It's a private school and getting a place at all is a problem because the school is over-subscribed. If only the state system could provide such ADHD-user-friendly education! I really believe that this, more than anything else, would cut the truancy rate. If school became a pleasurable experience for teenagers, they'd want to go!

I feel so deeply for Barney, and Adam too. I never realised how lucky I was with my education until we had Barney. On the whole I was very happy at school. I loved the challenges and I loved learning. I realise now that the teaching was presented to me in a way that I could learn, and that my rewards came frequently and easily. I could go to school each day and expect pleasure from lessons. It's not the same for Barney. He gets frustrated, fails and gives up sometimes. He goes to school and endures - day after day. He is lucky that he has such a happy-go-lucky, sunny disposition, and as a result I think he copes better than the majority of kids with ADHD. But as time goes on, as with any child who has ADHD, the gap between him and his peers increases, so the endurance becomes even more painful. Barney does have strengths. He's good at PE and drumming, and has a lovely treble voice, but because of his concentration problems and the way his school is run, these talents aren't being properly recognised or developed. And neither can they be unless the school changes its system. We can't change Barney. He is who he is.

I found school a user-friendly place and succeeded most of the time. But not every subject played to a strength of mine, I did have my Achilles heel. It was ART! Top in maths and bottom in art! I can't draw to save my life. And when I think about how I felt in art lessons it helps me to understand better how Barney must feel in most of his lessons except

PE. Sometimes I imagine what would have become of me if we'd all been forced to express ourselves 95 percent of the time through art, rather than through the written word at school. I can imagine reading and writing lessons having the Cinderella slot, rather like art has in many schools. I would have gone crazy having to draw, sculpt and pot to record or express what I had learned. I would have become very frustrated and ended up in a lot of trouble. This I am absolutely certain of as, in the last year of primary school, I *did* become frustrated and got into trouble. I found the speed of delivery far too slow, and the teacher couldn't feed me extra work quickly enough. I turned my mental abilities into pranks which, while they amused my peers and me greatly, were not in the least appreciated by the staff. If my frustrations had continued I would have eventually been expelled. But I went on to a grammar school where I was more stretched - and stretched by subjects in which I could succeed. It is no wonder that so many kids with ADHD and dyslexia end up being excluded and later, if the anti-social behaviour continues, in prison. This is one of my main fears for Barney.

A National Neurology

Barney goes to our local middle school and is swamped by the one-size-fits-all system where 'inclusion' is the idol before which all must bow. I know that in theory his work is meant to be differentiated according to his ability, but differentiating his work-tasks doesn't generate a sufficiently different teaching method, more suited to his neurology. He still has to put up with a curriculum which is based on his weak subjects. He's very unlikely to end up as an academic. Why try to press him into this mould? The National Curriculum is all very well, but I think that a National Curriculum will not be appropriate unless and until there exists a National Neurology.

What do I mean by a National Neurology? Well, it's something that doesn't exist. It would mean everybody having a brain with identical, or at least very similar, tendencies - everyone naturally learning in the same way as everybody else. It is Sean, Barney's educational psychologist, who's helped us to understand all of this. He's definitely ahead of his time. Or is it that he's plain old-fashioned, but simply uses the modern jargon? I am sure that with educational theory, as with everything else, 'there is nothing new under the sun'.[18] Anyway, Sean thinks the government will eventually realise how important it is to provide a whole range of schooling opportunities so that children with what he calls 'neuro-educational' or 'neuro-developmental' needs can have a much improved access to a curriculum with which they can cope, without being over-stressed. Sean was the person who helped me to see that suitable teaching methods and opportunities for children with ADHD and dyslexia should be focused on their strengths. He drew my attention to an American book with a story in it which illustrates beautifully what I'm trying to explain.

The Animal School

Once upon a time, the Animal State, having decided that education should be compulsory for all species between the ages of five and 16 months, set up a school. It was agreed that the curriculum should include

*running *climbing *swimming *flying

All animals were required to take all subjects, since it was politically correct to practise inclusion, regardless of the natural aptitudes of the different creatures. It was also decided to give a standard assessment test to all pupils at regular intervals.

The Duck obtained Grade A in swimming (and was even better than the instructor), Grade C in flying, Grade D in running and Grade E in climbing. Her webbed feet became badly worn from running, so her swimming grade eventually dropped from an A to a C. An average grade C for swimming was quite acceptable to the school authorities, so nobody worried about it - except the Duck, whose self-esteem and overall enjoyment of school life began to plummet.

The Rabbit, at his first assessment, gained a Grade A for running and was top of his class. However, he soon had a nervous breakdown because he was made to attend extra lessons in swimming in order to improve upon his low grade.

The Squirrel excelled at climbing (Grade A) and also did well at running (Grade B). But he became extremely frustrated at the school because the flying-class teacher forced him to start from the ground up instead of from the tree-top down. Consequently he persistently failed all flying tests (Grade F), whereas he knew that he could at least have achieved B+ if he had been allowed to do it his way. In addition, his climbing grade fell to a C and his running to a D. His doctor diagnosed him as suffering from a severe anxiety disorder, which had not been evident at the pre-school medical.

The Eagle came to the school as a reasonably happy pupil. Problems arose when, during the climbing classes, he beat all the others to the top of the tree but had insisted on using his own way to get there. He was labelled as suffering from conduct disorder and severely disciplined. Firstly he was made to stand on one leg outside the head teacher's study, and then he was forced to eat his lunch out of school.

At the end of the school year, the star pupil, gaining the head teacher's award, was an abnormal Eel who could swim exceedingly well, and could also run, climb and fly a little.

The Fox's parents withdrew him from the school because the administration refused to add digging and burrowing to the curriculum, even though they conceded that he might have a special need to do this. His parents were by then at their wits' end, since education was, by law, compulsory. Fortunately they happened to meet, and were very impressed by, the head teacher of another school, who was an open-minded Badger. Although his school was privately run, they felt that they had no option but to send their son there, joining an assortment of stoats, hedgehogs and sewer rats, and incurring an enormous cost to themselves of 12,000 chicken bones per year.

[Adapted for a British audience by Anna Richards, 1999, (based on a story in Chapter 22, 'Learning Disabilities', in Fundamentals of Human Neuropsychology, Fourth Edition. By Kolb, Bryan and Wishaw {1996})].

Are Barney and his ilk disabled?

Are these kids with 'neuro-developmental needs' what most people would call 'disabled'? It's a vital question. Do children with dyslexia and ADHD have a disability? And the answer, I think, is both 'No' and 'Yes'. In that order. No, they're not disabled when they're born. Both of the conditions can affect human beings right across the IQ spectrum. They can walk, talk, think and survive quite satisfactorily as they grow up. Some, particularly the dyslexics, are highly gifted in some areas. It could be in art and science like Leonardo da Vinci, or mathematics and physics like Albert Einstein, or diplomacy and science like Benjamin Franklin. Then there are the highly successful actors who have ADHD like Jim Carrey and Robin Williams. Winston Churchill too almost certainly had ADD and dyslexia and did appallingly badly in his early years at school. Interestingly, it is thought that Churchill took amphetamines - stimulant medication similar to Ritalin - during the war years, supplied to him by his American friends.

These children are not born with a disability as such. And yet ADHD is a potentially highly disabling condition that can lead to disastrous personal and social outcomes when mishandled or misunderstood.[19]

Because our society is so extremely biased towards the non-ADHD mentality, children with ADHD, as they grow up, find themselves to be misfits, and the first and most-extensively experienced area in which they don't fit is our education system. Because it is rare for these kids, or more precisely their parents, to find a school which is appropriate to their neurology, they become disabled, and for as long as they are forced to remain within such an educational system, they are disabled. So it's our society which disables them. If we did teach children with dyslexia and ADHD in a way by which they could more easily learn, and if they did have a curriculum suited to their abilities and strengths, then they would hardly be disabled at all.

Cruelty

A child can't simply change the way his brain functions. He or she can't, by an act of will, by trying harder or 'being obedient', magically change into a non-ADHD or non-dyslexic person. You might just as well expect him to change eye colour by sheer persistence! I don't think people realise how cruel the current system is. It's criminal too, but the powers that be simply don't realise this. If people realised this, the NSPCC would be inundated with telephone calls and letters. I believe that our society has a legal as well as a moral obligation to help these children. Almost 10 years ago the United Nations Convention on the Rights of the Child came into being, and our own government ratified this convention a couple of years later. The 23rd article of that convention states that if a child is disabled, either mentally or physically, he or she has the right to special care and education to help them grow up in the same way as other children. This isn't happening yet for children with ADHD or dyslexia as I've been explaining in this letter. Their rights are being denied, and in the process they are being abused.

So this is where you and the NSPCC come in, Jenny. Please read and pass around to your committee members the enclosed booklets about ADHD. If we can get the NSPCC to champion the cause of kids with ADHD, we might well be on the way to getting their extraordinary and complex needs met at long, long last.

With very best wishes,

Anna

Chapter 14

Wet Conditions

"There is no such thing as bad weather; there is only bad weather gear."

(Akela)

I glanced at my watch.

"Help. Look at the time! And this is supposed to be a walking holiday."

I leapt up out of my chair. "Where are the boys?"

"I'll take you through to the snooker room," said Jenny, calmly. The boys were still playing happily. Snooker brought out the best in Barney – if he played fast. He knew and knows no other way of playing any game. He has a knack of playing his shot with very little forethought, yet he succeeded in potting a lot of his shots. He seems able to quickly take in a visual image of the balls on the table and to respond rapidly to this information. He enjoyed the physical sensation of the impact of the cue-tip on the ball and this reward would be reinforced by frequent 'pots'. The rapidly changing patter of balls and successful shots keep him on task. If only his educators could tap into this aspect of his neurology – he'd be the class star!

With some effort Jenny and I managed to separate the boys from their game. We made our way to the farmhouse door, to where our boots and rucksacks awaited us.

"Good heavens! What a huge backpack you have!" Jenny commented as she eyed the towering blue cylinder which extended from the top of my legs to a point just a little higher than the top of my head.

"Sleeping bags," I explained. "I'm carrying two complete sets of bedding for Barney, as he has a problem with enuresis...bedwetting."

"Oh!" said Jenny, looking slightly embarrassed at first, but relaxing as she realised it was not a taboo subject as far as I was concerned.

We thanked our hostess for her kind change of heart towards us and for her much appreciated hospitality, each boy in turn speaking very politely. I was proud of them all.

"Please remember to post me that information!" she cried.

"I won't forget!"

And so we took our leave of Mile End Farm, making our way from the muddy farm track onto the even muddier footpath, now taking a route which was not part of the original plan. We had to make up for lost time and go for the best route to Tappenham, one which was interesting, direct and free from traffic. I led. The boys followed. Already the fine grey mist was developing into a veritable shower.

∞ ∞ ∞

Brain, bladder, praise and reward

Although he was 11 years of age, Barney still wet the bed. What amazed me was that we had been sent to one clinic to see a consultant paediatrician about Barney's ADHD and to a completely different clinic in a different town to see a different paediatrician about his enuresis. This went on for years. No-one seemed to realise that his brain and bladder were connected. During this time Barney made no progress whatsoever. It wasn't for want of trying, though.

The first method we had to try was 'praise and reward'. We were given a chart with boxes, one for each day – week 1, week 2, week 3 et cetera. For every dry night we were to give him a tick and lots of praise. Every time he was wet we had to put a little dot in the box. When he gained a certain number of consecutive ticks he would be congratulated at the clinic, receive a certificate of dry-bedded competence and be discharged. I don't know what the dots were meant to represent. I think it was a way of making the smallest possible mark on the chart so that the child did not feel too great a sense of failure. Barney's chart had so many dots on it that for me they came to represent streaming water droplets, symbolic of the Chinese water torture. We tried to 'up' the rewards and went through any and every available frippery that caught his interest and was affordable - football stickers, pogs, coins (of low value) - you name it, we tried it. Result? Drip, drip, drip, drip.

The electrical buzzer and X-ray

Next we tried the amazing electrical buzzer device. Barney had never been given such a fun toy in all his life! He very soon discovered that he could set the alarm off by peeing on the special mat and also by touching together the electrodes which connected the buzzer-box to the mat. This, as you can imagine, was infuriating – for us – but not for him. Buzz, buzz, buzz, buzz, buzz...Why didn't he get fed up with the noise? We did. Some nights he would eventually fall asleep with the device still intact and switched on, then when he weed he set the alarm off and continued to lay in bed, either awake or asleep, not taking any notice of the buzzer.

The condition of the buzzer got worse and worse. Barney dragged the relatively heavy electrical component along by its flimsy wire, causing the two pieces to part company. Aaron soldered it back together. In the end, the very delicate foil electrodes on the mat perished from a combination of mechanical friction and the chemical effects of urine. We conceded defeat. It cost us £25 to replace the battered machine and Barney went back on the little white cards and tick boxes...and there were more and more dots.

Then he saw the consultant paediatrician who diagnosed ADHD and prescribed Ritalin tablets. The result? Tick, tick, tick, tick in the boxes. It was amazing. Ten dry nights in a row. At Barney's next visit to the enuretic clinic he was presented with a certificate and discharged. But for no apparent reason the dots began to reappear on the chart and we returned to the enuretic clinic.

Water and an antidiuretic hormone

We then tried a couple of other methods. One was to get him to drink large amounts of water during the day and very little fluid in the evening. It didn't work. We also tried him on some tablets which contained a synthetic form of a natural human antidiuretic hormone. It works by reducing the ability of the kidneys to make urine. Well, it should work, but it didn't seem to work with Barney, so rather than use medication which wasn't helpful we took him off the tablets. When we considered the years of clinic visits, time out of school and the stress of trying method after method without success, we decided the time had come for a totally new approach.

Attitude, effort and reward

The biggest problem, we realised, was in our own minds. We were products of a society in which bedwetting is considered undesirable, almost unacceptable, to be cured quickly by whatever means possible, regardless of whether the child can control the function or not. Enuresis has been considered a problem for over 3,000 years. Egyptian records going back to 1550 BC suggested a 'cure' of cypress mixed with juniper and beer. The results were far from reliable. It doesn't matter where you live in the world, enuresis affects 17 per cent of five-year-olds, seven per cent of seven-year-olds and five per cent of 10-year-olds. Only relatively recently has it been realised that for children and adults with ADHD or ADD the proportion is much greater – between 40 per cent and 50 per cent.[20] Put that way, Barney is really quite 'normal'.

We didn't, and still don't know, whether Barney can do much about it. My theory is that, like most human behaviour, it is to do with the balance of reward and effort. Most of us hate the idea of wallowing in urine-soaked sheets so that the 'reward' of keeping our sheets dry will eventually rouse us from our warm beds and carry us to the loo in good time. Going to the loo does not require great effort. But for Barney, who has considerable difficulty organising himself, it must take great effort to get up from a nice warm bed, proceed along the landing to the toilet and pee in the right place. Even if we place a bucket by his bedside it rarely gets used. Barney frequently lies in a sodden bed without complaint until he is ready, for his own reasons, to get up for the day. It really isn't such a 'big deal' to him. I think his 'impaired' sense of time plays a part too. I suspect that he can't imagine that one minute of relative discomfort will earn him a long time in a warm, dry bed. He can't predict that the cost will be small for a reward which will be great. The future means very little to him.

It is also possible that his body still retains something of the Spinal Galant reflex which should have been inhibited by the time he was nine months old. Retention of this primitive reflex commonly results in the child continuing to wet the bed above the age of five years. [21]

Barney can't always control his urination and that can be embarrassing. The cure? Mop up, refuse to be embarrassed, and get on with life. Compared to the other problems associated with raising a child with ADHD, washing the sheets pales into insignificance.

Our bodies will let us down from time to time. St Francis of Assisi described the human body in a way which I find most enamouring. He calls it 'Brother Ass' (that is 'Ass' as in donkey, not as in 'Attention Surfeit Syndrome'!). C S Lewis has commented on St Francis' comparison in a particularly enchanting way:

"Ass is exquisitely right because no-one in his senses can either revere or hate a donkey. It is a useful, sturdy, lazy, obstinate, patient, lovable and infuriating beast; deserving now the stick and now a carrot; both pathetically and absurdly beautiful. So the body. There is no living with it till we recognise that one of its functions in our lives is to play the part of buffoon. Until some theory has sophisticated them, every man, woman and child in the world knows this. The fact that we have bodies is the oldest joke there is".[22]

The cost of bedwetting

The London Enuresis Clinic estimates that the annual cost of extra laundering and bedding comes to around £500. But I would maintain that this can easily be reduced by cold-rinsing the sheets together with a little disinfectant if desired, then spinning - rather than applying a full, heated washing programme on every occasion. One leaflet on enuresis states that bed wetters are united in almost always living in mortal fear of being discovered. Terrified to sleep over at the homes of others, they use elaborate measures to hide their problem.[23] This is understandable but tragic. Since we have become more laid-back about the whole thing, so too has Barney. A few extra sleeping bags which unzip to form duvets and fit inside a washing machine cost us between £1 and £3 each from a charity shop. They dry out quickly when well spun. Armed with these, a waterproof sheet and a black bin liner, the world is our oyster! When Barney is a bit older, we will try again to cure him of this affliction, unless of course he has grown out of it in the meantime. I have recently read about a body-worn enuresis alarm.[24]

All sorts of useful information is also available from the Enuresis Resource and Information Centre (ERIC). It is a UK based charity that gives advice and support on all aspects of childhood bedwetting as well as daytime wetting. (See www.eric.org.uk)

∞ ∞ ∞

I was jolted out of my thoughts by a sharp squall. The light shower had turned to real rain. The boys did not look happy. Up went their hoods. Down, deep into their pockets, went their hands and they hunched forward against the rain.

Barney had insisted upon wearing a more-fashionable jacket rather than the cagoule which I had advised. He was paying the penalty. I don't know whether he regretted his decision. Some youngsters would, so I have been told, rather die than appear 'un-cool' in the sight of their peers. We trudged on through the rain.

always managed to find long, slender branches – some flexible, some stiff – from which to make bows and arrows. And they work! If he didn't shoot the poor beasts he would stun or kill them with stones. When we play cricket and he deep fields he gathers up the ball in an instant and in the same movement can sling it with frightening accuracy at the wicket. Substitute rock for ball and wild animal for wicket and his potential is obvious. Thus Thom Hartmann's alternative perspective makes it difficult to view ADDers as having any kind of defect or deficit. True, they are terribly handicapped in the kind of society which we have engineered over the centuries, but in themselves, in their own way and milieu, they are stars. If they can capture their own talents, with help if necessary, the results can be astonishing.

Barney the Gatherer

ADDers are also good gatherers. Barney amazes us with the things that he picks up, mostly from the ground. His most frequent acquisitions are coins. We often joke that he'll never need to get a paid job - he could live off the money which others have dropped. Our daughter, Laura, once dropped a 'Yale' key which belonged to a friend. All we knew was that it was somewhere between our house and the other house, several hundred metres away. Barney found it in long grass. Translate this skill into finding berries and nuts and again we begin to see what enormous food-gathering potential this little person has. The problem for him is that he has no outlet for these skills in modern-day Britain. We buy our food at Tesco where hunting skills are redundant. Gathering skills might still have their place, you would think, but it is hardly a challenge to find the cornflakes on the same shelf in the same aisle every time.

Hunter-Gatherers versus Farmers

Hunting and gathering appeals to the 'now-time' mentality of the ADDer too. If you see a beast and kill it, in a society without refrigeration it will mean that meat appears on the table today. If you see nuts on the trees and fruit on the bushes, all you have to do is stretch out your hand and, hey presto, you have your food now. In contrast to this, farmers have a typical ASS mentality. A farmer has to be able to think ahead – to hope, wait and trust. A farmer has to sacrifice good seed and have the confidence to place it in a little hole in the ground, and then wait for months until a harvest can be gathered.

In most parts of the world today, society is characterised by farming. Meat is obtained by rearing rather than by hunting: cereals, fruits and vegetables by cultivating rather than by gathering. Our activities are heavily biased to favour ASS rather that ADDer neurology. Little wonder that so many people with ADD or ADHD feel different and out of place. In Thom Hartmann's book entitled *ADD – A Different Perception – 'Hunter in a Farmer's World'* he quotes Will Krynen:

"As a physician I've worked among indigenous hunting societies in other parts of the world, from Asia to the Americas. Over and over again I see among their adults and children the constellation of behaviours that we call ADD.

Among the members of the tribes of Northern Canada, such as the caribou hunters of the McKenzie Basin, these adaptive characteristics – constantly scanning the environment, quick decision-making (impulsiveness) and a willingness to take risks – contribute every year to the tribe's survival.

These same behaviours, however, often make it difficult for tribal children to succeed in Western schools when we try to impose our Western curriculum on them."

Hartmann suspects that ADDers now form the minority of the population because they have been systematically eliminated by the increasingly 'successful' ASSes who have plundered their environment, driving them out, and occasionally slaughtering them, in the process. Consider, in particular, the indigenous populations of North America, South America and Australia, and their present plights.

We are not slaughtering ADDers in modern Britain, but we certainly discriminate against them. In some cases we make life so unbearable for them that their misery leads to depression, or the depression which so frequently accompanies ADHD anyway is exacerbated. Depression sometimes leads to suicide in these cases; they slaughter themselves.

Those with ADHD today can be described as hunters who have lost their prey. We see it in Barney. He's bursting with energy, but there are no wolves out in the park for him to shoot, no bears to stone. Within the home, his equivalent activities are leaping around all over the place, tearing the house to pieces, or sitting in front of a computer screen 'zapping' as many aliens as possible. Outside, his antics are viewed by neighbours as being anti-social and disturbing, although most of them are perfectly innocent.

One reason why the English public boys' schools instituted the 'games cult' (organised sport), in a big way around 150 years ago, was to manage the antics of the ADDer boys. It was common for some of the pupils to spend their free-time away from the school premises hunting and poaching.[25] Sport was seen as an organised, viable alternative for these hunter-types. We should learn from the past. It is also interesting to note that when, in the late 1800s, the government was trying to enforce compulsory education, it proved most difficult to do so in the countryside, where children were engaged in activities of a hunter-gatherer kind, such as bird-scaring, gleaning and stone-gathering.[26]

ADHD in other species?

Human beings are not alone as a species in having hunters among its population. Take our dog, Tizer, for example. She is a cross-bred hound – a product of a beagle and a sheepdog. Consequently, she exhibits many characteristics of a 'hunter' dog. She can respond very quickly to the presence of other animals such as rabbits, cats, squirrels and deer in her environment. She is eight years old, but she behaves like a puppy – she is grossly immature. I am convinced that she has the doggy equivalent of ADHD. When I take her to the park she is noticeably more active than other dogs. I have considered giving her a Ritalin tablet to see what the effect is, but have so far resisted. I don't want to risk injuring her, and in any case we all love her exactly as she is. However, I still can't help wondering whether Ritalin would cause her to behave more like a laid-back and pensive labrador.

∞ ∞ ∞

As I trudged on across the field, with the boys behind me, our country walk seemed to be very unexciting. In fact, the boys seemed miserable, for the dark-grey clouds had descended upon us and once more pencil-leads shot down relentlessly from the sky. We had no ammunition to return and could only be helpless victims becoming steadily drenched. But, as so often happens after a particularly heavy shower, the cloud did eventually pass, unveiling a reddening, low, winter sun. In the east a beautiful rainbow appeared which took my breath away.

"Look!" I pointed.

"A rainbow," said Adam, seemingly unimpressed.

Aesthetic appreciation cannot be taught, only caught. Yet the boys were in no mood for catching anything...except perhaps a cold. I hastened the pace to get them warmer.

"Come on lads. Left, right, left, right. Just between those houses there and then we'll be in Kiddlewick where we can make our telephone call."

There was no telephone box. I checked the map again. I checked our position. I checked the road. No box or kiosk and definitely no telephone.

"It looks like Dr Who has beaten us to it." I said.

"What?" Lee looked very puzzled, as if he thought I was slightly barmy.

"Dr Who. You know. The TARDIS – a telephone box which just disappears into thin air. I know his was a police telephone box, but it's the same principle," I explained.

"So what do we do now?" said Adam, glumly.

"There's no alternative. Since there's no-one out and about, I'll have to ask at a house where the nearest telephone is."

I chose the house in front of us. It looked as good as any, and there was a light on. It was dusk. I pressed the bell and footsteps approached. A man in his late sixties opened the door and looked us up and down with a mixture of suspicion and amusement. We were wet and bedraggled.

"I'm very sorry to bother you," I apologised, "but we can't find the public telephone which is marked on our map." I waved the map in the air, as if by way of proof. "Please can you tell us where the nearest phone box is?"

He seemed to believe us, and if his expression had been faintly suspicious, it no longer was.

"Oh, British Telecom came and removed that telephone some while ago. Apparently not enough people were using it."

"Oh dear." I nodded sadly. "That's another penalty we're paying for having an out-of-date map."

"You're very welcome to come in and use my 'phone if you like."

I thanked him, explained who and why I needed to call and warned him that I might have to make two calls – one to tell the warden that we wanted an evening meal and to get the menu, and a second call to inform him of our choices. He looked bewildered, but resigned. Obviously he had never stayed in a youth hostel in his entire life.

We agreed that only I would go in and that the boys would remain outside. I removed my boots and he led me to the 'phone. I had the number of the youth hostel handy and punched it out.

"Tappenham Youth Hostel!"

"Hello, it's Anna Richards, ringing on behalf of our family group which is booked in tonight. There are only four of us, I'm afraid. I'd like to book us all an evening meal."

"Just in time! What would you like? There's mushroom soup or fruit juice for starters, followed by pizza and chips, tuna and macaroni vegetable bake, or baked potato with chilli and salad. Then for dessert there's ice-cream, yogurt or apple crumble and custard."

"I'll ring you back in a few minutes with the order!"

Tip-toeing past the man, self conscious of my damp feet, I smiled at him and thanked him yet again as I went out to the boys and described the choices for the evening meal. Their eyes lit up. Morale rose rapidly.

"Pizza and chips for me! And soup too!" said Lee, eyes a-sparkle.

"Same for me, except fruit juice not soup," said Adam.

"I'll have the same as Lee," said Barney, making his decision in the easiest way possible, and we all chose apple crumble and custard. The thought of a hot, stodgy pudding covered in steaming custard seemed like heaven. There were smells of cooking coming from the kitchen nearby, and we were all hungry.

My second 'phone call confirmed the details and I thanked our host again. He seemed to have stood motionless and watched my comings and goings between the telephone inside and the boys, in silence. Whether he felt amusement, annoyance or horror was impossible to tell. We took leave of him and headed out of the village towards the canal. I looked at my watch. I realised that it was going to be difficult, very difficult indeed, to reach the youth hostel by seven o'clock in time for our evening meal.

Chapter 16

Darkness by the Canal

"Education is the art of forming children into happy and useful men. One of the last and most perfect productions of the human mind will be a complete system of education."

(David Williams, A Treatise on Education, 1774)

"The light at the end of a tunnel is at the wrong end." §.

(Anon)

"OK lads, torches out, chocolate in!"

We had stopped by the edge of the canal as daylight finally faded. Our rucksacks lay on the grassy verge. Adam and Lee rummaged through their packs for their torches while I extracted cereal and chocolate bars, a headlamp and Barney's torch. I handed out the edible energy-boosters (alias morale-raisers). Lee began to wave his torch around in the misty air like a searchlight or lighthouse beam. Barney followed suit. Adam was still rummaging in his backpack.

"I need to plug it in," he said at last.

"You what?" I wondered whether I had heard correctly.

"I need to plug it in," repeated Adam. "It's rechargeable."

To my utter astonishment Adam was silhouetted against the sky, torch in right hand, three-pin plug in left hand with an electrical flex dangling between the two, as if looking for a socket.

"It needs recharging," he explained.

I took it from him and examined it. Never in my whole life had I seen a torch quite like this one. There, in the romantic setting of a canal after sunset, was my rude introduction to this contraption. I took it from him. I was convinced that some vital component, like batteries, was missing.

"Adam, you've forgotten your batteries! When I said bring a torch, I meant bring a torch which has batteries in. Next time I'll have to be more specific I can see, and say 'Bring torch with batteries, bulb, switch and electrical connections all in working order!'" My sarcasm was lost on him.

"But it has got a battery." Adam was adamant.

I flicked the switch back and forth, just as he had done. Nothing happened.

"Oh well, we'll survive. Can you swim? Yes? Good. You might need to if you fall in the canal for want of light. I think the best thing will be if we walk close together, even hold hands if you can bear it, and share the beam from my headlamp. Barney and Lee, you walk behind us with your torches." It was settled without complaints. We set off.

The stillness of the water was both eerie and beautiful. We kept conversation to a minimum and concentrated on keeping to the towpath. As time went on darkness closed in on us. We could easily have been walking through a tunnel. There was no visibility to the right or to the left of our torch beams. 'Tunnel vision' was all that we had. But then I was becoming accustomed to walking along dark tunnels, metaphorically speaking.

∞ ∞ ∞

One of the longest, darkest tunnels we have encountered, and one which Aaron and I were still walking through, was the one which addressed Barney's problems at school. We were not alone. Edward and Susan, Adam's parents, were having the same experience. Almost all parents of a child with ADHD find their child's education a confusing nightmare. We were all in darkness. We knew that things were going wrong at school for our children – badly wrong. But we had little idea of how to put it right, or even what exactly it was that we should be trying to achieve. It was like being trapped in a tunnel and spun round and round by forces beyond our control, leaving us giddy and totally disorientated.

As mentioned earlier, Barney's education took a major turn for the worse when he changed from the one-teacher one-classroom set up of lower school to the situation at middle school, where he had many teachers working in many different classrooms. The same had happened to Adam. Though both he and Barney had had some problems at their previous schools, these were not considered to be of an educational nature. Rather, they had been seen as behavioural issues - lack of concentration and distracting others as well as themselves. Teachers would report these things to us, implying that we should get our sons to change their unruly ways. Since they were not actually stupid, the situation would then become quite acceptable from an educational point of view. In other words, our sons were not seen as candidates to go on the special educational needs register.

Aaron and I didn't even know that such a register existed until we went to visit Barney's main class teacher at his middle school, by which time he was already nine-and-a-half years old. We were grateful, in retrospect, that the class teacher had invited the Special Educational Needs Co-ordinator (SENCO[#]) along. Many parents, we have since discovered, don't hear about SENCOs for a long time.

Lantern No 1

When we saw Barney's class teacher and SENCO we were very fortunate in that we already had a medical diagnosis for Barney. We knew that he had ADHD so the cause of his problems was not as baffling as it might have been. This, one could say, was the first light which we had to help us navigate through the educational needs tunnel.

Lantern No 2

The SENCO was helpful and sympathetic, and put Barney on the SEN register. She gave us a booklet entitled *Special Educational Needs – A Guide for Parents* published by the Department for Education, another light to guide us. The booklet was very helpful. It explained that there were five stages# on the special educational needs register.

Black Hole No 1

Barney's problems worsened. His school bag spawned utter chaos, if there was anything in it at all. His handwriting seemed to have deteriorated terribly. Now that various structures which had been in place in lower school (like lined paper, and the teacher writing the date on the board for children to copy) were no longer in place, Barney's schoolwork seemed to fall apart. It was as if he had coped at school up to then because his weaknesses had been supported by some kind of invisible framework – an 'exoskeleton' of sorts, rather like a child with a weak leg having it guarded and supported by a caliper. But once the caliper was removed, collapse followed.

We re-visited the class teacher and SENCO in the Autumn term of 1997. It was a terrible meeting. We seemed to be moving along a curved tunnel, the lights we had been given were now behind us, casting less and less light as we negotiated each bend. During that meeting at school we encountered three cruel twists, plunging us into increasing darkness. The first was the class teacher telling us that Barney was "not the worst" and that there were other children "far worse than he was". This left us feeling confused. What did other children have to do with it? Surely it was Barney and his problems that we were talking about right now. Wasn't it?

Black Hole No 2

The second cruel twist was when the SENCO explained how little help we could expect from the LEA because Barney's condition and characteristics "did not fit the boxes" on the form supplied by the LEA [27]. And she had a point. She told us the kinds of categories which would elicit extra help, and none of them really described our son. This meant that the LEA's form discriminated against Barney at the outset.

Black Hole No 3

The third cruel twist in the tunnel was when the SENCO told us that on top of it all, the LEA were desperately short of educational psychologists, to the point where Barney probably would not be seen for years, even if she put in a request there and then.

I'm quite sure that every parent of a child with ADHD or ADD in mainstream education has had dark moments such as these. And not just us, but most parents of children with dyslexia too. What do we do? Where can we go? Which way shall we turn? What is our goal? Do we even know what the light at the end of the tunnel looks like, and would we recognise it if we saw it? As Barney's education deteriorated we laid aside our socialist 'no private healthcare for us' principles and employed a private educational psychologist (Sean) to examine Barney.

Lantern No 3

Of all the people we have met in the dark tunnel of Barney's educational needs, Sean has provided us with the most light. He talked with us for a long time before he examined Barney, explaining much about the workings of the human brain. Sean then spent a whole day testing Barney, giving him frequent breaks to do as he pleased – run about, eat biscuits and have a drink – whatever he needed to do in order for the little lad to be able to keep going for so long. Sean's reports have helped us more than anything else to understand our son. It is only by understanding Barney as much as possible that we have been able to help him. Sean gave us great light to help us continue our journey, and we will always be profoundly grateful to him for that.

Black Hole No 4

Another 'twist' in the tunnel, darkening the surroundings further, was the discovery that the rule book which the LEA uses to assess a child and his or her needs is very thick indeed. It is most daunting. The full title is the *Code of Practice on the Identification and Assessment of Special Educational Needs.* Although I call it a rule book, apparently the 'Code of Practice', is not law. However, schools and LEAs must have regard to the Code of Practice, and if challenged at tribunal, they would have to have a very good reason indeed for deviating from it.

Lantern No 4

This Code of Practice turns out to be a two-sided coin. On the one hand, its mere appearance can plunge you into darkness and despair. On the other hand, if you manage to understand it, it can become your brightest lantern. It may be your deadliest enemy but also your greatest friend.

Why is it a friend? For two reasons. Firstly the Code of Practice really is on the side of the child. It maintains that a child's SENs should, if not must, be met, and it gives instructions as to how to go about getting them met. Secondly, it is a friend because it arms you against being fobbed off by the school and/or the LEA if your child's needs are not fully identified and understood. The school or LEA might claim that there isn't enough money in the pot to give you what you are asking for. However, the Code makes it quite clear that the child's needs must be met so, provided that you make it clear to them that all you are requesting is that his needs are met, you can always stick to your guns. The big problem, of course, is understanding the Code of Practice – of really getting to grips with it.

When I did finally grasp it, it was as though a giant floodlight was switched on in our tunnel. I remember it so well. It was a misty day in November 1998. I was visiting an elderly aunt in Bexhill-on-Sea. The journey by train and back took many hours. I took nothing to read but the Code of Practice, determined that its contents should not defeat me. When I boarded the first train that morning the Code was little more than gobbledygook to me. When I got off the last train that evening, I'd cracked it!

Lantern No 5

Some months earlier, back in the Summer of 1998, we had discovered that even if the school refused to put Barney forward to Stage 4# (because he didn't fit the little boxes on the form) to be assessed for being given a Statement of Special Educational Needs#, we could make such a request to the LEA under Section 329 of the 1996 Education Act. We did this on the basis of Barney having a medical condition, and referred to the Code of Practice (1994) Sections 3:89 to 3:92 in particular. It was vital to our case that Barney had already been officially diagnosed as having ADHD by a consultant paediatrician to whom he had been referred by our GP. If you are trying to use the assessment procedure in part to determine whether or not your child's special educational needs are underlain by ADHD, then you could find yourself in a Catch-22 situation. You may find it very difficult to persuade the LEA to do an assessment in the first place because you have no firm medical grounds on which to base your request. At the same time, your child's school, like ours, may, for whatever reasons, be refusing to make the request themselves. The result? You're stuck. The way out? Go to your GP and ask for your child to be referred to a consultant paediatrician. If your GP refuses then keep changing your GP until you find one who will, and in the meantime write to your member of parliament to inform him or her of the situation.

In Barney's particular circumstances the LEA were suitably convinced that we had grounds for requesting an assessment. The fact that we had a very thorough report from an educational psychologist, Sean, also supported our application. I am concerned about the little chance someone might have who has not been able to afford the £200-plus which such a report costs.

In July 1998 Stage 4 went into action. By December Barney had been 'statemented'. However, it had not been straightforward. In fact, we had had to get the LEA's initial decision, in November, to give Barney a 'Note in Lieu of a Statement'# overturned and changed to an actual statement. The difference between the two documents is significant. A 'Note in Lieu' merely gives advice to the school and has no legal status. A school could ignore it completely. On the other hand, a statement must be implemented, by law, and frequently specifies that some money is to be provided to make implementation possible. I am convinced that our negotiations with the LEA, which resulted in their change of heart, were only possible because of our knowledge of the Code of Practice and our understanding of ADHD. I had read many books about ADHD by then. I had been to a conference and studied all the latest research. It paid off.

We were thrilled when Barney's statement was finally agreed, and even more so when it was implemented. It was as if our tunnel had become brightened with Blackpool's illuminations. The main difference in Barney's education was that he was to be provided with a one-to-one Learning Support Assistant (LSA)# for seven hours per week. We did wonder how he would survive for the other 16 academic hours weekly, but it seemed far better than no extra help. Only time would tell whether the statement was 'hitting the nail on the head' or not.

The Shrouded Lantern (The IEP)

Since Barney had been at Stage 2# of the SEN register, there had been a particular lantern available to assist us through our journey along the educational tunnel, but we didn't notice it for a very long time. This lantern is the Individual Education Plan (IEP)#. I think we were unaware of its existence and potential because nobody drew our attention to it. I have since met several parents of children who are at Stage 3# and have not even been informed by the school that their child is on Stage 3, let alone know anything about their child's IEP. When I have suggested to them that they ask the SENCO for a copy of their child's IEP, and they do, it is remarkable how an IEP is rarely produced immediately, but instead the parents are told that they will be sent a copy the following week.

The IEP should be tailor-made for each child, as the adjective 'individual' would imply. This plan details specific targets which the child should reach by a set date. Parents have a right to be involved in its construction, and should not sign it if they are not satisfied. So far, Aaron and I have never felt able to sign any of Barney's IEPs because they have not made provision for an alternative curriculum based on Barney's learning strengths. Neither have the targets, in our opinion, been 'SMART'#. Targets should be 'SMART'. So what is meant by a SMART target? Like many words these days 'SMART' is an acronym. It stands for Small, Measurable, Accessible, Realistic and Timed.

When you check your child's proposed IEP (from the SENCO), my advice is always check that targets are SMART. If they are not, then, provided that it is in the child's best interests, insist that they are made SMART. Only sign an IEP if you know that you would be completely satisfied with your child's education if these SMART targets were to be reached. If at all possible get an educational psychologist to check the proposed IEP and offer his or her advice. If, when the agreed IEP is implemented, the targets are met, everyone can be happy. If they are not met, then you have solid grounds for the child to be moved up a Stage until, if necessary, Stage 4 is reached and assessment for a statement comes into operation.

Removing the shroud from this lantern and exposing the potential of the IEP as soon as possible will aid you in your journey.

The Lantern of Perpetual Comfort (The Named Person)

In the Code of Practice we learned that we were entitled to have a so-called 'Named Person'#. Usually a named person appears on the scene when the child reaches Stage 4, but I can't see any reason why you would be forbidden to have such a person helping you as soon as you are aware that your child has special educational needs. A Named Person can go with you to any meeting which you have with the school or LEA.

One of the best things we have done so far in our struggle to get Barney's special educational needs met, is to have invited Maggie to be our Named Person. To our immense joy and relief, she accepted. Maggie travels with us through the tunnel of darkness and provides us with light a lot of the time, and comfort at all times. We are amazingly blessed in having her to help us. She is a friend who has worked in the education sector. She has been the headteacher of an inner-London primary school in which many of the pupils had special educational needs. To 'crown' Maggie's suitability as a named person for Barney and us, Maggie has first-hand experience of teaching our son in a group setting in the Sunday school. She is able to provide us with valuable insight into the whole situation. Knowing that we can lean on her and that she is there to weep and laugh with is a continuing source of consolation to us. Most importantly of all, her presence at meetings almost certainly adds strength and persistence to our struggle.

Others – friends and colleagues who have children with ADHD but who have no named person – are being fobbed off left, right and centre, not just locally, but all over the country. They are making noticeably less headway than we are in a given time period. My advice to any parent who has a child with special educational needs is to take a named person or other witness to the meetings which you have with the school or LEA. Having such a person in attendance is a warning to anyone who would treat you unfairly or who would unjustifiably label you as a troublemaker. And even when you are fortunate enough to be in a meeting with officials who do genuinely want to help your child, your named person can be an advocate for your child while you draw breath and have time to order your thoughts. Having Maggie to be and do all this for us is a lantern that we would not want to be without. Thank you Maggie!

Black Hole No 5

Time went on into the summer months. Barney's statement had been in force for about six months. Disappointingly, we hadn't been able to detect any dramatic improvements in Barney's schoolwork. The real shock came when we attended a parents' meeting at the school and discovered, by asking the teachers directly, that although every one of them knew Barney was statemented, a large proportion of them had never read his statement. Only one or two out of about 10 teachers had their own copy, which they could refer to whenever they needed. We were appalled. How could a statement be implemented properly if the very people who were in the front line, so to speak, did not know precisely what it said? It also emerged at that meeting that Barney was continuing to have significant problems staying on-task in many of the subjects for which he had no support. We realised that Barney's statement wasn't providing all that we had hoped for. I had been continuing with my reading and research into ADHD, and discussions with experts and 'sufferers' alike. I understood more about ADHD than I had done previously and also more about Barney himself since the time that his statement had been written. It was clear that the statement which he currently had was quantitatively and qualitatively inadequate.

Quantitatively – the seven hours one-to-one support was insufficient. It left him free to roam either physically or mentally for the rest of his time in class.

Qualitatively – having a one-to-one LSA, untrained as a teacher, was not 'scratching where Barney itched'. Although she may have been doing an excellent job within her terms of reference, she was having to keep Barney on-task in academic subjects which were not his forte, and merely helping to squeeze him into a mould which, by nature, he did not fit. With no disrespect, and I have no proof, I suspect that there must have been times when all the LSA could do was provide a glorified babysitting service. I am virtually certain that Barney wasn't being given appropriately differentiated work to do all of the time. Despite the statement, the school did not have the human resources available for this. It is no criticism of the school, but rather a criticism of a system which promises to meet a child's special educational needs but which in practice, is unable to do so. Inclusion is the name of the game, but as Barney's educational psychologist has said – maximum inclusion means maximum differentiation. Barney's statement made no provision for the adapted or alternative curriculum which he needed.

The Flickering Lantern (writing letters to Barney's school)

A lantern which flickers is good news at one moment, and bad news the next. Writing letters to Barney's school is proving to be like this. All the official advice is for parents, teachers and medics to work together for the good of the child. Working together requires excellent communication, so writing to the school should be good news for everyone concerned. In a letter, you can write exactly what you are trying to convey.

At the receiving end the school has a chance to respond in its own time (though promptly, we hope), without risk of a knee-jerk reaction or an ill-considered response. Thus the lantern can be bright and illuminating to all concerned...or so it should be.

As it turns out, this method of communicating was not welcomed by the school at all. The lantern flickered and then went very dim.

Most of our letters went unanswered. The school informed us that we were writing too many of them. I explained that one reason why our letters were increasing in number was because our earlier ones had not been replied to, and when I asked if any of our letters had been unreasonable in their content, and if so which, the school was unable to name even one.

We were told that as things stood the staff were being very patient with Barney, but if we kept on writing letters, then the situation might change. Was this a threat? It sounded like one. Moreover, the school then told us that certain members of staff (unspecified) were wondering just what our agenda was. "Our agenda?" I gasped. "Our agenda? Our agenda is to ensure that our son gets the best possible education. What else would it be?" That they had even asked the question shocked me deeply. Why was the situation between us and our son's school deteriorating in this way?

From our perspective all we had done was try and make matters clear, whether we were giving information to the school, or whether we were asking for information in return. Perhaps it was getting too much for the school, we could understand that: caring for and teaching a child with ADHD will push you to the limits of your time, your energy and your endurance.

Let's suppose the school was doing its best for Barney. If so, then it demonstrates how unreasonable it is for the government to expect an ordinary mainstream middle school to properly address the highly complex and demanding special educational needs of a child with ADHD. And if this is so, then the sooner the school openly and honestly admitted it, the better.

While letters are necessary, they are easily open to misinterpretation, however much care one takes to phrase them well. Letters cannot convey body language; there is no smile to show that while you may be serious about the content of what you are saying, you still wish to remain on good terms with your opponent. Opponent? Did I say 'opponent'? Yes, opponent. For that is what the schools and LEAs become. It is the common experience of almost every parent I know whose child has ADHD.

So letters, far from enhancing goodwill and assisting communication, actually cause the school to clam up and resist. The dim lantern has flickered again, and then gone out.

Black Hole No 6

We were plunged back into the darkness again. Nevertheless, we continue to write letters. Why? you might ask. To be provocative? No! We continue to write them not only for the reasons already mentioned, but for legal reasons too.

Our sole aim is to get an appropriate education for Barney, but we were finding a considerable degree of resistance from the school and the LEA, be it deliberate or accidental on their part. It was possible that at some stage we might have to go to tribunal to appeal against a decision made by the LEA which we believed was not in Barney's best interest. We wanted to be properly equipped at any hearing – our chances of success would be reduced if we were without carefully presented documentary evidence.

Black Hole No 7

In October 1999 we were entering yet another section of uncharted, poorly-lit tunnel. Adding to the gloom, it had become clear that the LEA was not monitoring the school's implementation of the statement. Apparently it does not have enough money to carry out such monitoring. So much for a statement having legal teeth, as we had previously thought. We have called for an early review. As we walked in darkness by the canal that night, I reflected that the review was only 10 days away. I wondered what would happen next...

Yet we were the lucky ones. We had come far. As time went on I was meeting more and more parents with children who had ADHD/ADD and/or dyslexia who either knew nothing about the five-staged approach to meeting SENs, or who had hit a 'glass ceiling' at Stage 3 and seemed to get no further. We were all frustrated – parents and children alike. The children were landed with an educational system which they found difficult to access, and we parents were landed with children whose gifts and strengths were not being developed, and who were demonstrating the consequences by various types of antisocial behaviour: loss of motivation, fear, embarrassment, procrastination and depression. If only their creative thinking and visual style of learning could be developed. If only the characteristics of ADHD could, as Thom Hartmann so clearly points out, be viewed as assets rather than liabilities.

It is unacceptable to force ADDers and dyslexics to learn in ways that are at odds with their nature. It is as outdated and ludicrous as insisting that left-handed children use their right hand for writing. It used to happen and in some places it still does.

Sir Laurens van der Post relates an incident which occurred in the early 1960s when he was travelling in Russia. He was visiting a 'model' boarding school in Tashkent. The schoolteachers showed him around, demonstrating with pride their language laboratories, where teachers and pupils practised reading from the English and American 19th Century classics. As van der Post was about to leave the school, he asked a simple, perceptive question which seems to have thrown his hosts into confusion.

"Incidentally," I asked the teachers who assembled to see me off, "what do you do about teaching your left-handed children?"

They looked dumfounded until one of the Russians said brusquely "We have no left-handed children, here or anywhere else."

The attitude implicit in this dismissal of what is a universal educational problem drove home the point. Neither a left-handed child nor a left-handed spirit nor a left-handed nationalism had place in the future for which this education was a preparation.[28]

One can well imagine an equivalent scenario happening in Britain today. An American journalist visits our mainstream schools and when he is on the point of leaving one of them, he poses a question to the staff and headteacher.

"Incidentally, what do you do about teaching your children who have ADHD?". They look dumbfounded until one of them says brusquely: "We have no children with ADHD, here or anywhere else."

The attitude implicit in this dismissal of a universal educational problem drives the point home. Neither a child with ADHD nor a spirit of ADHD nor a nationalism which includes ADHD has a place in the future for which this education is a preparation.

My one consolation is found in reflecting upon what has happened in Russia between 1960 and 1999. We have to fight on for Barney.

Aaron and I have spent several years living and working in West Africa, and looking back on this time we are both grateful now for the extreme conditions which this continent provided in teaching us to stand our ground when we were confronted by bureaucrats and uniformed officials. It was a very tough battlefield indeed. The 'offences' which we were alleged to have committed, and against which we had to defend ourselves, ranged from the trivial to the bizarre. On one occasion our crime consisted of permitting the tax disc to fall off the windscreen of our pick-up truck. Another time I was harassed for trying to take a child's doll – hollow, plastic, naked and black – out of the country to give to my young niece as a gift. On a different occasion we were arrested because the exact dosage of cholera vaccine registered on our health certificates was illegible. What doctor ever does write legibly? Most bizarrely of all, I was once taken aside by a customs officer who found my applicator-free tampons. Only the most delicate and persistent persuasion on my part secured my eventual release (after all, I was fully aware that what I was saying did sound rather implausible!) But my insistence that these items were not rounds of ammunition was eventually accepted.

Standing up for Barney's rights against the British bureaucrats of education (apart from a few notable exceptions) often feels like a repeated experience of these less than pleasant African times. Confronting those teachers, headteachers and LEA officers who try to use their status to intimidate is both tedious and exhausting. It is infuriating when they are more than happy to let Barney tick along and even fester in an inappropriate educational set-up, just because Ritalin has quelled his more disruptive side. Silly, pathetic excuses – so confidently delivered – are thrust before parents of children with ADHD as if to overawe us and cause us to back off. Those repeated arguments of "There are other children worse than yours", and "There's not enough money to go round", can be intensely annoying. How come there's enough money to educate our children inappropriately but not appropriately? Facing these British authorities is, I suppose, child's play compared with standing up to the uniformed West Africans. After all, when did you last see a British headteacher or education officer brandishing a gun?

So, we will battle on, inspired by the late, great Sir Winston Churchill:

"We shall not flag nor fail. We shall go on to the end...we shall fight with growing confidence and growing strength in the air...we shall fight...we shall fight...we shall fight. We shall never surrender."

Chapter 17

A Ride on the Tappenham Omnibus

"The boy was in disgrace. He sat locked up in the nursery of Agathox Lodge, learning poetry for a punishment. His father had said, "My boy! I can pardon anything but untruthfulness," and had caned him, saying at each stroke, "There is no omnibus, no driver, no bridge..."

(*The Celestial Omnibus* in *Collected Short Stories* by E.M. Forster)

Sometimes, looking back, it seems like a dream. Pitch blackness can have a strange effect on the mind. In all the time that we walked in darkness along the canal, not one of the boys expressed any signs of discomfort, fear or misgiving. They simply and quietly lapped up the sense of adventure and concentrated on where they put their feet. With a canal on our left and some kind of fence, wall, hedge or other boundary on our right, there was very little possibility of wandering off-route. I was well aware that all this would change the moment we reached the road and searched for the next set of footpaths which would take us cross-country to the youth hostel. The beam of my headlamp caught the side of a bridge which passed over the canal. It was a road bridge, and gave us a definite map position. The quickest way to the hostel would be to walk along this road. However, traffic was always a danger, especially at night. On the other hand, if we took a cross-country route our path was bound to be ill-defined across muddy fields. In pitch darkness it would be very slow going. Time was pressing on mercilessly. It would not be long before supper was served.

We clambered up some steps which brought us onto the road. I swung my beam around to establish whether or not the road had a footpath, or even a pavement running alongside. It did not.

Rona, a Scottish friend of mine, spoke to me some years ago about God answering prayers that she had never even got around to praying. Such amazing 'unprayed prayers' as I like to call them – more usually known as coincidences – have unexpectedly punctuated my own life several times. I remember one such incident in January 1978 when Aaron and I, still newly-weds, were living and working in Nigeria. My front teeth broke in a complicated way which could only ultimately be fixed by my home dentist in England since he had moulds of what my teeth had originally looked like. A series of temporary fixes in Nigeria (including Araldite which we later found out was poisonous) all failed. So it was arranged that I would fly home for two weeks to get the whole dental project completed. One minor problem was that all of our sterling currency had disappeared – presumed stolen. This meant that when I landed at Heathrow Airport I would have no money for the fare to my parents' home. Nobody was able to collect me from the airport. Nevertheless, this was the least of my worries compared to the ordeal of getting through customs at Kano Airport while flatly refusing to pay a bribe for any of the ridiculous reasons presented by the customs officials.

My flight was booked with KLM, Royal Dutch Airlines, and necessitated an overnight stop in Amsterdam where I was accommodated in a swish hotel somewhere out in the wilds on what was probably a polder. It was dark when I awoke, and with time to spare I decided to go for a walk in the countryside. The weather was cold, dank and misty. When I reached the furthest limit of my morning stroll and began to turn back, dawn just breaking, my eye caught a square black object lying on the ground. How I managed to spot it in such poorly-lit conditions, I shall never know. I picked it up. It was the simplest kind of wallet imaginable, extremely tatty, and very definitely on its last legs. I opened it. Inside was a crisp, new twenty-five guilder bank note, in mint condition. The curious thing was that it was quite dry.

What should I do? Take it to the police? I wasn't sure of the value of twenty-five guilders. Maybe I would be wasting their time. In any case, what police? I didn't have time for any of that; I had a 'plane to catch! What about the hotel? It would be pointless handing it in there; the find had not taken place on their premises. Rapidly I came to the conclusion that the obvious solution was simply to keep it - pocket the money, thank the Good Lord for His provision, and run! At Heathrow the 'Bureau de Change' was happy to exchange my Dutch money for a five-pound note, and I arrived at my parents' home by public transport a couple of hours later. The whole thing was quite extraordinary.

"Who would have been so stupid as to pray for a thing like that?" Rona would say to me in her gentle Scottish lilt. What she meant, I think, was 'Who among us has the faith to believe that God would so order events as we would like, even down to the finest details?' But were they 'unprayed prayers'? Although I might not have got round to praying, how can I ever know whether someone, somewhere else in the world had been praying for my well-being?

Barney, Adam and Lee stood beside me on that road in the pitch black, waiting for me to give the next set of instructions. Barney saw it first.

"Look Mum! There's a bus!"

I did look. I could hardly believe my eyes. The road over the canal narrowed to single-width at the bridge. A set of traffic lights controlled the passage of vehicles - not that we had seen even one vehicle so far. But there, over the far side of the hump-back, was the glare of a large pair of headlights. My eyes accustomed themselves to this apparition. Unmistakably it was a bus, stationary. The driver and a few passengers were now visible and, most striking of all, the destination board showed 'Tappenham'. It was like a dream. There was no time to lose. The bus was held up, obviously by a red traffic light, and the lights could change at any moment.

"Wait here!" I shouted to the boys and sprinted to the bus. To gain the driver's attention, I knocked on one of the long door panels. He pressed a button somewhere and with a hiss the panels opened. The driver looked at me, surprised and dubious.

“Hello!” I said cheerily, “We’d like to go to Tappenham Youth Hostel - do you pass close by?”

“This isn’t a bus stop,” came the retort.

“Oh? Isn’t it?” Sometimes mock innocence works wonders. On this occasion it was plain that rather more skilful dialogue would be necessary before he might invite us on board. I was just about to continue in my most-polite voice with my most-winning smile and ask “Then please would you mind driving ever so slowly so that we can run as fast as we can to the next bus stop and reach it before you do...” when I was saved the bother. The three boys, unable to restrain themselves any longer, had caught me up and leapt on board! The driver’s jaw dropped. He could see immediately that he was up against an unstoppable force, shook his head slowly, rolled his eyes heavenwards and belatedly said “Come on in then”.

The boys joyfully sprang onto some seats. I fumbled through my rucksack for some money.

“Never mind the fare,” said the driver as he pulled away. “There isn’t a bus stop here so I don’t know what it would be anyway.”

“Oh thanks! That’s really kind!” I said, and joined the boys.

Anybody who lives in rural England knows that the public transport system is generally poor and at worst, non-existent. To have come across a bus to Tappenham at any time of day or night would have been surprising. To intercept one when in such great need was nothing short of miraculous. I thought of Rona again saying “Who would be so stupid as to pray for a thing like that?!” I smiled and thanked God for his mercies.

Streetlights loomed ahead out of the darkness. There were pavements, houses and a pub. The bus drew to a halt. The doors hissed again. We tumbled out, each of us thanking the driver as we passed him, descending the steps. The doors hissed one final time, shut, and the bus accelerated away. By now it was twelve minutes to seven. Barney and I were old hands at youth hostelling. Lee had been once before to a hostel so he would know roughly what to expect tonight. As for Adam, it was all new. We entered the back door of the hostel, offloaded our damp clothing and boots into the drying room and headed for the reception desk.

This particular warden, like most youth-hostel wardens, was very kind. Although there were now only four of us occupying the five-bedded dormitory which we had booked, he waived the fee for the fifth bed. How pleasant it would have been if I could have simply deposited the boys in the male dormitory and escaped to the sanctuary of the female one. If only...

Our room was on the top floor. Inside were two sets of bunk-beds and, under the window, a single bed. Each boy staked out his territory immediately, claiming the bed of his choice and ‘bagging’ it by flinging some article of his clothing upon it. We just about had time to don some dry clothes and wash our hands before going downstairs to an immensely welcome evening meal. How good food tastes when you have walked for it! How comforting are the four walls and roof of a building when you have battled through wind and rain. How reassuring is the light in each room when not long before you were travelling in darkness. These simple creature comforts were not lost on any of us, and we gratefully tucked into our dinners.

∞ ∞ ∞

Body temperature and its maintenance

One of the big attractions of staying in a youth hostel for Barney is the chance to have a shower. At home our bathroom ceiling pitches steeply making it impossible to install a shower cubicle.

Barney loves hot water – passionately. Conversely, he detests cold water. Trips to the local swimming pool have always proved difficult. It is usually only possible to persuade Barney to go into the pool at all if there are some of his friends present. At the first opportunity he will bolt from the pool and dart into the men's changing room, staying there indefinitely under the hot shower. Many has been the time when I've had to ask the male life-guard to remove my son from the showers and return him to me.

At home, particularly in the cooler months, we have a similar situation with the bath. Every morning Barney needs one, because of his nocturnal enuresis. He likes the water to be piping hot – far hotter than I can take. It is impractical to police him all the time when he is bathing that early in the day, since there is so much to be done. As the water cools, Barney tops it up with more hot water until the entire hot water system is drained. In addition to this, he goes crazy with the bath foam. It's not unusual for me to return to our house, having given the dog her early walk, to find huge white masses of Tesco Value Bath Foam cascading away from our house like an ice-floe up and along the footpath. Hacking my way through this foam mountain, I eventually reach the door, enter and go upstairs. There sits Barney like Lord Muck, head poking through a sea of bubbles playing with the now empty plastic bottle, still occupying the bath even though the water has drained away. I keep meaning to transfer a small amount of bath foam into another empty plastic bottle for each day's use. Somehow I never get round to it. Maybe Barney isn't the only one with organisational problems in our house!

It's not just hot water which Barney craves, but hot radiators too. When the central heating goes on for the winter it's always easy to find Barney – search each switched-on radiator. If Barney is not actually plastered against one of them in spread-eagle style, he's bound to be nearby. This behaviour used to drive us mad when he was younger. Now that his educational psychologist, Sean, has helped us to understand why it happens, we find it much easier to accept.

Sean explained how body temperature is one of the most basic things that human beings need to maintain for our survival. I already knew this from my studies of human biology and also from mountain-craft knowledge, but had never thought to apply this information to Barney's curious behaviour. Apparently, whereas you or I if we are cold would consider remedying the problem by putting on a sweater, Barney, who finds this a highly demanding task, avoids solving the problem in this way if there is a simpler alternative. It is complicated and costly for him to think where the sweater is located, go

to that drawer, get the sweater, put the sweater over his head, left arm through one sleeve, right arm through the other and return to base. It's quick and easy to maintain his body temperature by clinging to the radiator. Q.E.D. It's common sense once you've seen it, yet it had us puzzled for years. I suppose it's another of those 'effort' versus 'reward' situations. For Barney, the effort involved in getting the sweater and putting it on is far too great for the reward of a raised body temperature, when there is an alternative option (the radiator) which costs far less effort. In fact, the necessity for Barney to maintain his body temperature as simply as possible may also go a long way in explaining his reluctance to get out of bed in the night to go to the loo.
It is usually cold out there, and much warmer under his bed covers.

∞ ∞ ∞

After we had all showered that evening, we wandered down to the lounge. Barney had been enticed out of his shower by the prospect of having fun downstairs with Adam and Lee so, thankfully, removing him from the shower hadn't been a problem. I was pretty tired by now and ready to sleep. The boys were not. There seemed to be no point in insisting on an early night. It made sense for the boys to enjoy themselves in the lounge for as long as possible. A very friendly family from East Anglia were just setting up a game of 'Risk' on the table. Adam liked this game. He asked whether he could play and the family immediately included him. That was one of the lovely aspects of staying in a youth hostel. Everyone who stays there is a member (or guest of a member), so everything is in some sense communally owned. There is very little sense of 'This is my game', or 'This is my book'. It is one of the few places in which I feel able to relax with Barney. If a cup or plate gets smashed, the warden isn't going to shed any tears over it. All the crockery is bog-standard light green anyway, and easily replaced. There are no Ming vases in the hallways.

Neither Barney nor Lee wanted to play 'Risk', which was just as well because by then the table was full with the maximum number of players. I smiled to myself. How apt it seemed that Adam, a child with ADHD, was about to play 'Risk'. Barney and Lee began to rummage through some kind of a toy box. Seeing that they were well occupied, I left the room and went off to the telephone kiosk to 'phone Aaron, exchange our news and confirm that all was well for him to come and collect us at nine-o'-clock the following morning.

Wearily, I climbed the staircase. Outside our dormitory, near the floor, was an electrical socket. Adam had wasted no time in finding it. His torch was plugged in. I switched the mains supply off, removed the plug and flicked the switch on the torch. It lit up immediately. So it did work! Somewhere inside the casing, despite its lightness, there must be a battery after all. I laughed, plugged it back in and let it continue to charge.

Already we had transformed the dormitory into a complete tip. The beds still had to be made up. Should I insist that the boys make their own beds? No. Making them myself would be my gift to them. They'd had a long day, been absolutely brilliant and deserved to enjoy their games downstairs uninterrupted. What I really meant was that it was easier this way.

Chapter 18

Crucifixion

"Continue to work with the faith that unearned suffering is redemptive." §

(Martin Luther King Jr.)

The noise was terrible, the conversation lewd. I had eventually managed to get the boys into their beds, but none of them remained there for long. Lee needed the loo again. Barney swore he spotted a spider crawling on the carpet in the area illuminated by the landing light which streamed underneath an ill-fitting door. He leapt out of bed to put the main light on, to search for it properly, by which time it had disappeared – if it had ever existed in the first place. Not knowing where it was caused him to fret even more. Adam was too hot and slung off his duvet. Barney decided that he needed an extra pillow - and so it went on. During all this activity they were having debates about various matters mostly associated with parts of the male anatomy and the covert antics of adolescent boys. They squealed, laughed and shouted. Barney and Lee continually fell out of their beds onto the floor and climbed back in again. It was as if I wasn't there - out of sight, out of mind. My orders and pleadings were heeded for five seconds at most and then it was as if they had never been given.

Adam was in the bunk above me and could not settle at all. He tossed. He turned. He flicked his torch light on. He flicked it off. On. Off. On. Off. I thought about the fact that the clocks went back tonight. There would be one hour's extra sleep. Correction: there would be one hour's extra torment, with me trying to confine these boys to this room. Was it a blessing or curse, this extra hour? I could not decide. But one thing was clear; right now it was hell. I couldn't control the boys and we ran a very high risk of receiving complaints from the other hostellers, if not from the warden himself.

It should not have surprised me that our hostelling trip wasn't a complete bed of roses. The moment I decided to throw in my lot with the ADDers for a day and a night, I was bound to suffer. I had no option but to endure.

∞ ∞ ∞

Pain, suffering, rejection and condemnation

Much as we love our children with ADHD, there is no doubt that their effect causes immense pain. Neither is there any doubt that the children themselves also suffer. Let's imagine that our darling baby is born or, like Barney, adopted. He looks absolutely gorgeous and even if he does not, he certainly doesn't look abnormal. He grows and develops and we expect a certain standard of behaviour to evolve. The reality is quite different. Our darling child starts to walk and never stops. He avoids eye-contact with us, shirks cuddles, battles desperately to get away, punches, kicks and bites. He eventually starts to talk - frequently in complete sentences. Although we don't often swear at home, he does. He has been born without a 'think bubble'. He suffers from 'OTM-OTM' syndrome – On The Mind, Out The Mouth. He can't internalise speech like most children do and whatever word comes into his head, goes forth from his lips. Whatever action seems good, is done without forethought – regardless of the consequences. We reject this difficult behaviour and live on the edge of rejecting the child himself. We become physically exhausted. We are forever clearing up messes, mending broken objects, replacing lost or destroyed items, apologising to friends, neighbours, relatives and strangers. One by one our social contacts are lost. Social leprosy sets in. We are permanently tired and stressed. Obsessive or compulsive behaviours, so typical of a child with ADHD, threaten to tip us over the edge. With Barney it was flicking light switches on and off, on and off, then pulling the joints in his fingers, feet and ankles. Later he started to repeatedly remove and replace the lids of pots and jars – click, click, click.

Other parents watch and let you know, either by their expression or more directly by their words, that they would never permit any child of theirs to behave in this way. Even your own parents, the child's grandparents, may disapprove of your failure to discipline him early enough. In desperation you take your child to the doctor. He might refer you to a child psychiatrist. The child psychiatrist insists on seeing the whole family together, perhaps having decided beforehand that the underlying problem is one of relationships. The possibility of a neurological problem, confined to the skull of the problem-child, may not cross the psychiatrist's mind. The fact that there is an older sibling in the family with no apparent problems is ignored. The parents are blamed, and since it is the mother who has been spending most of the time with the child, trying to get him to comply but failing, it is she who takes greater share of responsibility. Now, on top of all the other pain comes this added burden – the guilt of bad parenting.

I remember when all this happened to us. How shall I ever forget? When Barney was five he was referred by our doctor to a child psychiatrist, let's call him Dr X. As is so often the case with children who have ADHD, their hyperactivity miraculously disappears for the length of time that they are in the psychiatrist's surgery. Somehow the sheer novelty of the place sees to that. I lost confidence in myself as a parent when Dr X pronounced me to be a mother who failed to encourage her son adequately. It had been plain to Aaron and me that something wasn't quite right about Barney as soon as he had become mobile. As the situation deteriorated it was obvious to us that something was very wrong indeed. We had an older daughter who was behaving much as one would expect. Surely it made sense that the problem resided somewhere within Barney?

Living next door to us were two children, Vicky and James, just a few years older than our two. When they were young, the four children spent time playing together. Vicky was about nine, James seven, Laura five and Barney three when the three older children composed a rhyme about Barney, as if on his behalf. It went like this:

I'm Barney Mark Richards from outer space
I am not part of the human race
In my family I'm a disgrace
I'm Barney Mark Richards from outer space

They didn't mean to be cruel, I know. They were simply giving expression to their view of Barney in a concise, poetic way! Analysis of the rhyme illustrates the conclusions drawn by the three older children. Firstly, in some strange way, Barney did not belong to this world in the same way that most human beings do. Secondly, he behaves in a socially unacceptable way. Thirdly, the cause of his antisocial behaviour is tied up with his alien status. These children made a brilliant diagnosis. But why was it these young children, educated at local primary schools and earning nothing, were able to make a sound and reasonable diagnosis while Dr X, aged about 50, educated at medical school and earning a high salary, had failed? It is bizarre. As awareness of the reality of ADHD increases, I hope and pray that fewer child psychiatrists will miss this possibility.

In the time between our visit to Dr X in October 1993 and Barney's correct diagnosis by a consultant paediatrician in April 1996, a parody of the children's rhyme, as I imagined Dr X would have written, hung over me:

You're Mrs A Richards who's out of place
A failure in the human race
As a boy's mother, total disgrace
You're Mrs A Richards who's out of place

Stress

Much of the literature published by the Department of Education and Employment (DfEE – now DfES) and Advisory Centre for Education (ACE) about assessing children with special educational needs and getting those needs met, notes that this process is stressful for parents. It is refreshing to see this acknowledged in print. We found and continue to find the process of trying to get Barney's special and complex needs met a very punishing one indeed. We had to go to great lengths in terms of time, research, money and emotional stress before approaching the LEA ourselves when Barney's school proved unco-operative. There continued to be other considerable financial costs - stationery, photocopying, post, telephone, conference fees, books and especially loss of income as I set aside my career.

Without doubt, the greatest cost of all was to my personal health, and the consequent effects on the rest of the family, including my elderly mother. By February 1999 I had battled for two months with our LEA about the proper wording of Barney's statement. At least 14 of the learning difficulties identified by the assessment process at Stage 4 had not been mentioned in the draft statement, contrary to Section 4:27 of the Code of Practice. I became quite ill. The neurotransmitters in my brain ceased to function properly and, as many people know, this condition is commonly known as clinical depression. Thanks to a wonderful husband, family, GP and friends, I made a recovery. One outcome of this unhappy event was that I learned at first hand what life was like when one's powers of concentration are severely limited. It is hell. Yet this is what Barney and other children like him experience daily at school where so much is demanded of them, and so little is understood by those who surround them.

As a family we only just avoided complete breakdown. It could easily have ended in disaster, with only one functioning parent. It is not unrealistic to imagine both children eventually ending up in the care of social services.

Psyche battering

ADDer children go through their most formative years being yelled at and screamed at by human beings far bigger than they are. The words 'No!', 'Stop it!', 'Don't!', 'Get off!' batter their psyches from dawn 'til dusk, and beyond. When they reach the age of five they start school and for the next 11 years, almost every day they experience fear, frustration and failure. They are square pegs forced into round holes.

Cooper and Ideus at Cambridge University note that it is not unusual for parents and teachers to have become adversaries by the time a child's social and academic difficulties have progressed to the point where ADHD is being considered. They point out that in any partnership, the teacher-parent relationship, created to help the child, can sometimes be eroded through a cycle of anger, criticism and blame.[29] When Adam's parents removed him from his local mainstream school they said that they did it *"to prevent him from being crucified any further."* I will never forget those words.

Jerry Mills, an American teacher and songwriter now in his forties who has ADHD describes his experience of school as *"a bizarre descent into a living hell"*. At best, he was misunderstood. At worst, he was persecuted. Jerry sums up his thoughts brilliantly and succinctly in his song entitled *The Ones Responsible.*

The Ones Responsible

In my hometown there was a school that I attended as a child
Where I earned the reputation for bein' a little too wild
And even though I left that place over 20 years ago
The memories of it haunt me almost everywhere I go

I went there for nine long years, from kindergarten through eighth grade
And I wish I had a Dollar for every screw up that I made
Because maybe with all those riches I'd be able to make some sense
Of just what the hell was goin' on, what the hell was goin' on...?

Spare the rod and spoil the child, but why couldn't they just let me rot
Instead of having to endure all of the punishment that I got
For not payin' attention, for bein' the class clown
For not obeyin' orders when I was told to settle down
For forgetting to do my homework, for not bein' ready on time
For failin' to keep my way of life between their dotted lines
For 30 years it's haunted me until I figured out
Just what the hell was goin' on...what the hell was goin' on...

Heaven help the children who live their lives with restless, achin' souls
Always acting so impulsively and lacking self-control

Heaven help someone to change the children's nightmares into dreams
But God help the ones responsible...for destroying their self-esteem

It takes all kinds to make a world, and some can make the world unkind
But there's no one in this world with the right to blow a young kid's mind
By treating them like trouble instead of trying to figure out
Just what the hell is goin' on?
What the hell is goin' on?
What the hell is goin' on?

The Ones Responsible
From the recording *Urgent Reply*
(c)1993 by Jerry Mills
Reprinted with permission
For information contact www.jerrymills.com or jerrymills@aol.com

Jerry, amazingly, holds no grudges against his educators. He appreciates that, 30 years ago, things happened to him simply because of his teachers' lack of awareness. Today it is reasonable to expect that all teachers should be aware of ADHD, and have a responsibility to meet the needs of these children.

Fluctuations

One particular problem which Barney and all other children with ADHD face at school is the inevitable fluctuation in the quality of their work from day to day. It is characteristic of the condition that some days, even some *moments*, are better than others. One thing that can be said about children with ADHD is that they are *consistently inconsistent*! If the electrical connections in the brain are working well, the child can, during that time, produce work relatively effortlessly and on a par with his peers. If connections are bad, then work requires an enormous effort and, in spite of this, the results are of poor quality. Handwriting is often barely legible at times like this. The child's teacher cannot view the inside of his brain to see what the neurons and neurotransmitters are up to. What the teacher sees is what's produced on paper. Because the child has, at sometime, produced work of good quality, it is wrongly assumed that the child is always capable of working to this standard. The problem of inconsistency and unpredictability is frustrating and soul-destroying for child and tutor alike. Ironically, ordering a child to 'Concentrate!' usually makes matters worse as it causes the brain to disconnect even more. PET scans have revealed an increase in 'holes' – inactive areas of the brain where connections are failing to occur – when this order is given. This has enormous implications for educators.

Cooper and Ideus draw a very helpful analogy between ADHD and Cerebral Palsy (CP). CP is a neurological condition that affects the individual's ability to control his or her muscle and limb movements. Children with CP are prone to involuntary movements of their limbs, in the same way that children with ADHD are prone to involuntary shifts of their attention, involuntary expressions of their impulses, and involuntary motor activity.[30]

School reports

School report time and its aftermath is a demoralising and frustrating experience for all parents of ADDers, and for the children themselves. Time and again we have to suffer the indignity of comments which merely describe what our child has done, or ought to be doing but is not, in terms of the ADHD/ADD core symptoms. We don't need to be told that our child has concentration problems, organisational problems and is impulsive. We already know that. What teacher would ever dream of telling the parents of a blind boy that their son has a problem with his sight? or the parents of a deaf girl that their daughter has a problem with her hearing? Yet it is this reporting of symptoms that ADDer-parents have to endure constantly.

Consider these comments from the school reports of Barney, Adam and other ADDer children and reflect on how these reports would read if the children's problems were sensory impairment or physical disability:

Barney

"Barney must think before he acts as he has deleted his work by accident on more than one occasion...Barney must realise that self-discipline is the key to success and happiness at school. He must develop a much more positive attitude towards work and begin to recognise the value of concentrated attention."

[If blind] "Barney must look more closely at his work as he has failed to notice it on more than one occasion...Barney must realise that being able to see what he has done is the key to success and happiness at school. He must develop a much more positive attitude towards seeing and begin to recognise the value of clear eyesight."

Adam

"Adam has not made much progress this year, mainly due to his inability to concentrate. He is far too easily distracted. With greater effort I am certain that his skills in all areas will develop."

[If deaf] "Adam has not made much progress this year, mainly due to his inability to hear. He fails to respond to sound far too easily. With greater effort I am certain that his skills in all areas will develop."

Daniel

"The main target which we need to work on is the improvement of Daniel's concentration."

[If a leg missing] "The main target which we need to work on is the improvement of Daniel's ability to run."

Rory

"He is too easily distracted - he must try to concentrate. If he could remember to be properly equipped, his output would improve...Rory must work harder at good habits of organisation."

[If blind] "Rory too easily fails to see - he must try to look. If his vision was not so blurred, his output would improve...Rory must work harder at good habits of looking more closely at his work."

Pat

"Pat does not fully concentrate on the task in hand - she is easily distracted...She must ensure that she does not let herself get side-tracked...The standard of her work is inconsistent...Pat needs to develop work routines that will generate consistent results."

[If deaf] "Pat does not hear what tasks are in hand - she easily misses what is said...She must ensure that she does not miss oral instructions...The standard of her work indicates poor listening...Pat needs to develop work routines that will generate better hearing."

Alethea

"Alethea finds difficulty dividing fact from fiction...She shows immature behaviour in relation to her peers...She needs to develop her organisational skills and systematic thinking."

[If a leg missing] "Alethea finds difficulty standing up...She is much slower in games than her peers...She needs to develop stronger limbs and greater speed of movement."

A range of disorders and school exclusion

If ADHD continues to go undiagnosed and unaddressed, more complex, undesirable behaviours appear as the child grows. These typically include Oppositional Defiant Disorder (ODD)# and Conduct Disorder (CD)#. There are some 3,000 children permanently expelled from schools in the UK, with 8,000 children in residential homes because of 'emotional and behavioural problems'. Over two per cent of the child population are said to have a significant emotional and behavioural disorder. Frequently, the symptoms of the comorbid conditions are the most prominent entities drawn to the attention of the child's carers and the underlying ADHD is not fully appreciated.[31]

The child's worst enemy

No child enjoys being like this. It may appear to everyone that he has become his own worst enemy. It could be argued though, that his worst enemy is whichever adult – a parent, teacher, educational psychologist, doctor, social-worker, friend or relative – who, suspecting that ADHD could be the root cause of the problems, still fails to act upon that suspicion and initiate the necessary help.

Although it is negligent to ignore the symptoms of ADHD, I have some sympathy with those who do. I went through a denial stage when, in late 1995, I realised, when reading a book, that the evidence for Barney having ADHD was overwhelming. There is a strong desire, a little voice deep inside, which says "Oh no! Not this. Not ADHD. Please God, let it be something else – better still, let it be nothing at all. If it is ADHD then I'm going to have to do something about it, and I don't understand what I'm up against, or where it will end."

Fear can so easily get the better of us and paralyse us in the process. I put off the decision to approach our GP for several weeks. Thank God I didn't delay any longer.

Chapter 19

Journeys into Hell

"The road of good intentions is paved with Hell." §

(Spencer Ante)

A piercing shriek rent the air. I had thought that the boys were dropping off to sleep. How wrong can you be? Barney had landed on top of Lee's bed, no doubt crushing or banging some part of himself in the process. Whether he had dropped down from the vacant top bunk or simply launched himself from the lower berth, I am not sure. There was a scuffle and suddenly a ghostly-white bag appeared. It contained Adam's legs in the lower half of his sheet-sleeping bag, dangling and oscillating ominously over the side of the bunk above my head. Before I could say anything it dropped with an enormous thump onto the floor. BANG! CRASH! Adam lost his balance inside the sack-like shroud and toppled over sideways, out of control.

"Get off."

"It's not me."

"It is you."

"Aaaaaaargh!"

Raucous laughter, another shriek, and more disjointed exclamations were hurled into the night, no-one sure who was saying what to whom.

It was many minutes before I managed to regain any kind of control and get the boys back into their original beds. I was amazed that no-one banged on our door, or walls, to complain. Perhaps we didn't hear them. Eventually a semblance of peace was restored – always punctuated by some kind of rude noise, chortle, accusatory remark or squeal. Gradually the silences became longer. Things were settling down at last. Another noise from Adam. The bunk bed wobbled. More strange noises. It was clear that Adam was not able to control his strange behaviour.

∞ ∞ ∞

Adam, Edward and Susan's journey

Adam's parents, Edward and Susan, have tried so hard to get help for him, but have been fobbed off time and again. Like the parents of so many children with ADHD who are trying to get appropriate help for their child, they are now being vilified by the school and education authority alike. They are earning (unjustifiably) the reputation of being troublemakers. I have heard Edward referred to as a 'bully' and there have been half-joking comments about him having horns and a tail. He and Susan believe that these labels are being used to undermine their credibility so that the school and LEA can continue to perpetrate the notion that they and Adam have a behavioural problem rather than Adam having a genuine neurological special need. In addition to these difficulties comes the added insult, injury and indignity of being misunderstood and characterised as parents who are anti-school or anti-the-education-system. The truth is that they are attempting to demonstrate to the teachers the implications of ADHD as an 'invisible' disorder.

Susan has recently written a poem '*Whose Child?*' – poignant words which have arisen out of the depths of her frustration and anguish.

Whose Child?

We gave him life
We loved him
He grew from baby to infant
He explored and ran and went too fast
He wasn't one of the 'norm'

We needed help and advice
Of that we were given freely
"He'll grow out of it" was the cry
But did he? No, not nearly

"Be careful", "It's additives", "Hyperactivity"
"Don't push too hard, he will be labelled"
"Wait a while, he will settle down"
"He's a boy!". "Don't worry"
"We know what he needs – Discipline!"
Cried the school

Where was the care to find out for sure?
Whose 'duty' was it to find the cure?
We tried and tried to make you understand
That there was something wrong
We did know that
But what?
Who can help?
Why will no one listen?

Our right as parents diminished by laws
The 'school' blameless by protections
Beware it will happen more and more
Parent partnerships with schools have

A major flaw
The child who needs help will become
A statistic of a faceless number
The state takes him and if he doesn't measure up
Whose child?
Whose child?

Susan

(Mother of Adam, then aged 10, at that time undiagnosed as having ADHD)

An ADHD teenager's journey

If ADHD continues to go undiagnosed and untreated, by the time the child reaches teenage years it is virtually impossible to keep him playing nicely inside the home, doing his homework as and when told. He is very vulnerable to getting in with a bad crowd, very easily led and very prone to substance abuse and crime. Truancy is likely. The government talks about 'parent partnership' and about parents being ultimately responsible for their truant children. But how can parents reasonably be expected to get their youngsters to school, short of strait-jacketing them, or taking them there at gunpoint? Many of the children are bigger and stronger than their parents. Even fining the parents several thousand pounds is unlikely to change the impulsive behaviour of a persistent truant.

At the 2nd Annual ADD Information Services Conference, held in London in October 1998, Doctor Alison Munden, a Child and Adolescent Psychiatrist working at the Birmingham Children's Hospital, NHS Trust, presented the results of her study. The study had investigated ADD/ADHD and behavioural and emotional problems in children who had been excluded from mainstream education. Her study team found that excluded children had a very high incidence of ADD/ADHD and Emotional and Behavioural Disorders. Similarly, a survey of children in care in the Oxford Local Authority area showed that 96 per cent of children in residential care and 60 per cent in foster care had a psychiatric disorder.[32]

Many of these children and adolescents had ADHD which was unrecognised.

John Sanford, HM Prison Officer and parent of an adopted son with ADHD, also presented a paper. He said that 90 per cent of crime is committed by just six per cent of the population. He estimates that half of that six per cent have ADHD/ADD and do not know it. Obviously, not all people with ADHD will commit crime and become imprisoned, neither do all prisoners have ADHD. But the point is that unless and until every child who does have ADHD is appropriately and successfully treated – educationally, socially and where necessary medically, widespread crime-related suffering will continue.

Siblings and their hellish journey

One often forgotten group which may suffer greatly are the siblings of children with ADHD. Their hell may be different, but it may be just as acute. Many children report that they are easy targets for their brother's (or sister's) aggression because their parents are either too exhausted or too overwhelmed to intervene. They become very resentful of the way that family life is controlled by the sibling with ADHD. They yearn for peace and quiet and mourn not having a 'normal' existence.[33] Imagine what it is like for them when their toys are repeatedly broken, their vital possessions go missing and their personal space is trashed. The enemy is within the home. There is nowhere else to run. It seems unjust when the sister or brother seems to get away with behaviour which parents never tolerated from you, and just because little Freda or Freddy has this thing called ADHD. What's more, those annoying little brats (as they appear to the siblings) seem to get all the parental attention. Mum or Dad is always running around after them, - always trying to sort them out. "What about me for a change? I'm your child too! Don't I have a right to some of your time? You're always preoccupied with writing letters and talking to other parents whose kids have similar problems. It's not fair!" Then, to add insult to injury, you start to lose credibility with your peers at school because you have such a dork of a sister, or the most embarrassing brother in the whole world. It is also very worrying - the fear that your sibling with ADHD might get hurt by other people and get into trouble, is very real. Yes, siblings suffer too, and the extent of their suffering is not always recognised.

Homework – The spiralling journey of descent

As I think of all the stresses generated within the home in which there is a child of school age with ADHD, there is one particular demon which rears its ugly head repeatedly. Its impact can hardly be imagined by families who are blessed with compliant, educationally well-motivated children. The name of the demon is 'Homework'. Homework causes high levels of negativity and disruption. I know what this demon looks like and its other name is 'The Tyrannical Triangle'. It resembles a one-way spiral staircase with a triangular cross-section and three barbed points to each downward segment. On one of these barbs hangs the parent; on the next the impaled child, and on the last is the teacher. So, in a descending and painful spiral we find parent, child, teacher, parent, child, teacher ad infinitum. The demon 'Homework' is vicious and, as you cast your eyes down its ugly form, you will see parent, child and teacher gradually transformed into uglier and crabbier specimens.

Children with ADHD cannot or will not do homework. But **why** can't they or won't they do it? There may be a variety of reasons:

- the child cannot do the work
- the child can do the work but takes too long to do it
- the child is so disorganised he didn't even know he had homework
- the child did not remember or know when the work was due
- the child has multiple skill deficits
- the parent's role as parent and teacher becomes confused.[34]

Any of the reasons will result in the child becoming less and less motivated to do his homework. It becomes the worst chore in the world. The situation is made worse when the child has poor concepts of cause and effect. He can't appreciate the consequences of not doing homework, least of all those far off, nebulous ideas of 'getting qualifications', 'going to college' or 'getting a good job'.

It is wonderful if a child is motivated to do homework and does it by choice. But where the desire is absent and when the homework is piling up, this horrible demon can threaten to demolish whatever happy family life you might still possess. If the school insists on a child with ADHD doing homework, then they have an obligation to set up systems which allow for successful outcomes. Aubrey and Joyce Fein have set up schools in South Africa and North America in which they have devised a series of well thought-out ways of motivating pupils with ADHD to do homework. When I think of Barney, or Adam, I can see that pressure on our families would be reduced if the schools were to set up a supervised 'homework club'. It would be well structured and include breaks for exercise and snacks. Barney finds it much easier to do what all the other kids are doing than to go it alone, in almost any and every activity.

So, how do real families actually manage to cope in practice with this demon 'Homework'? Most of them struggle on and suffer increasing destabilisation of their home life. The parents of one young lad, Andrew, rather than cause upset with the school, are doing the homework themselves. Obviously, this defeats the whole purpose of the homework. The parents of Rory, Pat and Alethea have been driven to such distraction that they have decided to back off completely from any kind of policing of their children's homework. The consequence is that the children do not do homework any more. For some strange reason, the school hasn't said a word about this. Do they care or do they just want to let sleeping dogs lie?

When I had recovered from my clinical depression, I came up with the idea of employing James, who lives next door (now a bright young man in his mid-teens), to be Barney's personal homework tutor. We had to think it out well. The job is full of frustrations. We set the rate of pay at double that which his older sister, Vicky, earns at the local supermarket. It only takes James 10 seconds to travel to 'work', and we have limited Barney's homework to a maximum of half-an-hour per evening, so the 'end' is in sight for James, when keeping Barney on-task and motivated is proving particularly difficult. This system is working well. James is a form of 'novelty' each evening and this helps to gain Barney's attention. He is also a wonderful role-model for young Barney and a much more acceptable one than I can ever be. We know that James won't be with us for ever but we are grateful for the respite he brings us in the meantime.

Edward and Susan are following suit and hope to arrange for a homework tutor to help Adam. But these interventions cost money. We are supported by the Disability Living Allowance which we claim for Barney, and in spite of the complicated and lengthy forms involved, this is well worth considering in these or similar circumstances.

Now that we have James, can we say that the problem of the triangular spiral has been solved? No. That would be claiming too much. Barney frequently arrives home without homework instructions, or vital books and equipment, despite having a Statement of Special Educational Needs which states that staff are responsible for ensuring that all the necessary items are present and that parents know what has to be done. By involving James the problem has been lessened, but the demon 'Homework' is still with us.

The journey of denial by teachers

I think that one reason why ADHD as a possible cause of a child's problems is so frequently pushed aside by schools is because it still possesses an ambiguous status in our society. There remains a widespread suspicion that ADHD may not be a genuine condition but rather a pretext for poor parenting or teaching. Teachers and headteachers fear that they will be considered weak or looking for excuses, if they admit that they cannot control or make progress with a particular child. Whereas parents know that the children will be ours for life and we can no longer ignore the problems, in the case of a teacher or headteacher, all they have to do is to hang on and, eventually, the child goes away into another teacher's class, then ultimately leaves the school and takes his difficulties elsewhere. Two documents entitled *Classroom Management Strategies for AD(H)D Pupils* and *Strategies to Address Specific Behavioural Issues of Individual Pupils*,[35] give excellent advice but present a daunting and time-consuming task if they are to be thoroughly studied. No wonder some teachers are tempted to keep quiet about their suspicions. If they admit to them then they will be under obligation to implement the management strategies.

Sometimes I try and put myself in the position of a teacher of many years standing who has just become aware of the existence of ADHD and the enormity of its implications. I might well look back over my teaching career and realise that specific children I had taught, or tried to teach, were extremely likely to have had this condition. I would probably feel very guilty about the way in which I had treated these ADDers. The years and years of effort which I had put into perfecting particular teaching methods and materials might now seem inappropriate. Just one child with ADHD in my class now could threaten my whole way of working. I would be horrified at the prospect of having to change my entire way of teaching! The incentive for teachers to draw attention to the child's problems is not as great as it is for the parents. The greatest motivator to put every effort into the task is the love that the parent has for the child.

One of our closest friends is a secondary school teacher who admitted to me that she was certain a particular boy she was teaching had ADHD.

"Have you alerted anyone to the fact?" I asked her.

"Oh no. I literally haven't had the time," came the reply, "I can hardly manage to keep up with the teaching, let alone get involved with something like that."

Now this woman is one of the most caring, selfless and considerate people that I know. If she feels pushed into ignoring the problem, how much more so must the thousands of other teachers who are not as conscientious as she is. I often wonder if our friend had spotted the symptoms of meningitis in one of her pupils, whether she would have similarly failed to report it. The obvious answer would be 'No, of course not. Meningitis can be fatal.' But this is also true of untreated ADHD.

Fire-fighting the flames of hell

There are some very impressive educational books available which give excellent advice on ways in which schools can intervene and work with children who have ADHD. But if the majority of teachers are, like our friend, over-stretched by large classes and constrained by the demands of the National Curriculum, all that they can reasonably be expected to do is to 'fire-fight' and survive. They don't have the time or the means to 'fire-proof' the system. So, unless their employers take the initiative to completely refurbish the educational system with non-inflammable structures, then fire-fighting scenarios will continue to be played out in our schools. Thus the heartache and misery extend way beyond the children with ADHD, their parents and siblings, and include a large proportion of teachers, caught in the fiery hell of an educational system in which fewer and fewer people are able to find fulfilment.

Accidents and suicide – the final journey

Statistics show that adolescents with ADHD are four times more likely to be involved in a serious car accident, and also at far greater risk compared to their non-ADHD peers, of overdosing on drugs or alcohol, substance abuse, and committing suicide.[36]

I will never forget the mothers I have met of teenage boys and young men in their early 20s who had taken their own lives. These young men, although bright, had never got on at school. They had constantly been in trouble, totally blamed for their failure to conform and had school reports which read 'could do better if only he would apply himself'. ADHD had never been diagnosed nor treated in any way – their education never adjusted to suit their personalities, weaknesses and gifts. In the absence of stimulus or stimulant medication they self-stimulated on drugs, alcohol and glue-sniffing. In a world where the tune being called was one to which they could not dance, they had committed suicide. It was only later, in retrospect, that their parents learned about ADHD and recognised that their sons had been suffering from this all their brief lives. These brave mothers have stood up and spoken at conferences, determined that awareness of ADHD will be raised so that children such as these are understood, accepted and catered for, and that no more young lives are lost.

I thanked God again that Barney had a clear diagnosis and that already we had come a fair distance in addressing his special needs. But one great spectre remained - when, if ever, would we be able to solve the problem of Barney's education? We know the enemy which we face and we can look it in the eye. If we love our son we have to continue the battle to ensure that all his special needs, and most especially his educational ones, are met. Anyone who goes into battle can expect to get wounded. There will be scars, but, despite the scars, victory is always possible.

∞ ∞ ∞

The boys had settled at last. There was peace – just the gentle sound of a child's breathing. I prayed Reinhold Niebuhr's prayer:

Lord, give me the serenity to accept the things which I cannot change
The courage to change the things I can
And the wisdom to know the difference
Amen

Chapter 20

Resurrection and New Life...With a Vengeance!

"Weeping may tarry for the night, but joy comes with the morning."

(Psalm 30:5)

My wrist-watch sounded the alarm at seven o'clock – what used to be eight o'clock before we had set the clocks back. There was noticeably more light now than there had been at seven the previous morning. This was not only because of the change from British Summer Time to Greenwich Mean Time. Yesterday had been damp, dull and foreboding but today was cold, crisp and bright.

The alarm served two purposes. Firstly it woke me up. Secondly, it was the signal to give Barney and Adam their Ritalin. This done, they both scuttled out of the dormitory to join Lee who was already in the men's washroom. Alone at last. I thought. For how long would my privacy continue? Not long.

I had managed to get myself half-dressed when a piercing bell sounded, an alarm – the fire alarm without doubt.

"Oh no! Which one of them is responsible?" I thought.

On the back of every dormitory door, in every youth hostel, is a set of instructions 'In Case of Fire'. Grabbing a sweater, I yanked it on while scanning the directions. That done, I proceeded immediately to the courtyard hoping fervently that the boys would either be there already, or would arrive soon afterwards. I need not have worried. They soon appeared. Already there was a group of about 20 people in various states of dress and undress – men, women, boys and girls. One man was half-shaven! Others were still trickling out of the hostel, delayed no doubt by some vital bodily function or by a state of complete nudity when the alarm had first sounded.

The warden had evidently been outside longer than any of us. He was fuming, and not because it was a false alarm.

"You're too slow! All of you. Too slow! If that had been a real fire most of you would have been choking with smoke by now, if you'd made it as far as the door that is!"

A few more late-comers sauntered out and visibly started as the warden laid into them without pausing for breath.

"As for you lot, you'd be burning! Two minutes. Two minutes - that's all you've got if you want to keep your life!"

Some of the more scantily clad hostellers were shivering by now. Clearly, keeping us outside for longer was to be part of our punishment. Then, just as we thought it was all over, a sinewy gentleman of about 70 came tip-toeing out, clutching a black holdall.

"And YOU!" screamed the warden, pointing at him. "You'd be history. Dead. Ashes. Never, ever delay getting out for the sake of a bag when the fire alarm sounds!"

A little septuagenarian lady, clearly the culprit's wife, squeaked up.

"I told him. I did. I'm always telling him. He never takes any notice of anyone, not even me. And he won't take out any insurance either. I keep telling him."

Her penultimate sentence was something of a non-sequitur, but it spoke volumes. I stood, dumbstruck, amazed and charmed by this outplay of humanity in all its richness, culminating in the woman's personal revelation of domestic discord.

I did not need to ask which of the boys had done it. For some reason, all three were standing on a bench. Then I realised why. They had exited without shoes thereby, I presumed, earning the warden's approval. The fact that Barney almost never wore his shoes anyway was neither here nor there! Barney and Adam had been pointing at Lee, who showed no intention of denying it. In fact, quite the opposite. He seemed proud of his achievement. I suppose it had given him some kind of thrill associated with power to see so many people, mostly adults, caught in a state of undress and having to re-order their lives as a result of his actions.

"I thought it was the shower door. I did!" he claimed, barely suppressing a smile. Inside the men's washroom, apparently, was a fire exit. Enough said.

I suggested to Lee that he might apologise to the warden and to the people. To his credit he did, without protest. We went back into the hostel to get some breakfast. Rather than have the full cooked English breakfast provided by the warden, we chose to have a lighter meal of cereal and milk, supplemented by our left-over rations from the previous day's journey. We sat down to eat and ended up with the usual mess of pools of milk and granulated sugar spread across the table. No problem really. All could be wiped up. Barney wanted to finish off some apple tarts, so I went to the crockery shelf and grabbed a plate to give him. It never reached the table but slipped out of his hand and crashed onto the floor. To my astonishment and relief it did not break. It would have been particularly embarrassing having to confess another misdemeanour.

Barney had had a bad record of experiences with ceramic items. Seeing him drop the plate reminded me of the time (before he was diagnosed with ADHD) when his head teacher had called Aaron and me into school because Barney had banged another child's toy – some kind of ceramic object – so hard and repeatedly on the classroom desk that it had shattered into pieces. It had looked like an act of deliberate destruction, but Barney appeared to have had no understanding about how the breakage had happened at all.

What was it that compelled Barney, and many similar children, to behave in this way? I can only assume that the ritual satisfies some kind of neurological need. He must get satisfaction or relief from the physical act of contracting and relaxing his arm muscle repeatedly, from the thudding vibrations juddering through his body, from hearing the 'clack-clack-clack' sound as clay hits wood, or from watching as the object performs its rhythmic dance. To him this behaviour is not 'bad', it is neutral, like the smaller fidgets we ignore from other children.

Barney obviously took pleasure in bashing many different hard objects. When we take him mountaineering in North Wales, we often walk through a slate quarry where a peculiar obsession immediately possesses our son. He appears to be unaware of our existence and oblivious to discomfort from cold or rain. He crouches down, picks up pieces of slate and begins to smash them, systematically working his way through a pile, totally focussed on his task. If Barney had been working with flint it would be easy to imagine him as an archetypal junior caveman, trying out the most useful shapes for an axe-head or an arrow-tip. The 'hunter' within him is never far from the surface.

∞ ∞ ∞

Back in the members' kitchen no harm had been done. I picked the plate up from the kitchen floor, put it in the sink and replaced it with a clean one. Adam started talking about the game of Risk which he had played the previous evening. Apparently he had played well. I was certainly impressed by how well he had managed to concentrate for the entire duration of the game. He had obviously switched into his focussed state.

"You know the man?" said Adam.

"What man?" I asked.

"The one I was playing with, in that family."

"Oh, yes. I don't exactly know him, but I know who you mean. Peter, I think his name is. Stephen's Dad."

"He kept telling Barney and Lee off. He kept saying they were too old to play with the toys in the box, and told them to be quiet."

The beetroot in my Polish blood boiled within my veins. I was indignant! We were back to the same old problem of Barney not acting his age. His 'normal' appearance belied his underlying neurological differences and caused adults to expect far more from him than he was actually capable of. I tried to see it from Peter's point of view.

He couldn't know that Barney had ADHD, and even if he did, could he be expected to understand why Barney behaved so immaturely? Should I just drop the matter? It was tempting. But then there was the importance of justice for Barney and Lee. It was understandable to me that Lee, who liked action, had become Barney's accomplice. If the two boys were going to enjoy each other's company in the lounge and Barney, whose Ritalin would have worn off by that time, was in active mode, it would be the most natural thing in the world for Lee to join in the activity. But I also had to consider the matter of justice towards Peter, and tread very carefully.

I had heard a programme on the radio which featured an Indian boy and his mother. The boy was severely autistic but had come to the fore on account of his amazing giftedness as a poet. The mother had worked so hard with her son, helping him to fit into the world as well as possible. She had told him: "You must adjust to the world, my son, because the world will not adjust to you." I admired her tremendously. Her love, dedication and sheer hard work had achieved wonders. I applaud her effort and am sure she has done the right thing by her son. However, is it somewhat defeatist to say that the world will not adjust to her son? Changing the boy and changing the world are not mutually exclusive goals. Why won't the world adjust to him? Because of ignorance. The feelings and needs of people in wheelchairs have been far better understood and accommodated in recent decades than previously, through awareness-raising and education of the able-bodied, coupled with legislation. There is surely no reason why society cannot develop the same awareness and sensitivity to people who are autistic or have ADHD.

In a slightly different context, some 2000 years ago, St Paul wrote "Don't let the world around you squeeze you into its own mould".[37] No minority group should feel under obligation to fit the mould of the majority when the differences between them are genetic and not a matter of morals or law. I made a decision.

"Where is Peter now, do you know?" I asked Adam.

"I think he's having breakfast in the main dining room," he answered.

"Well, I'm going to have a word with him and explain about Barney and his ADHD. I think he ought to know, otherwise he'll never understand."

Adam's jaw dropped in amazement. He appeared to be simultaneously awed and excited at the prospect. He wasn't used to adults advocating on behalf of noisy children. Barney and Lee added their support, eager to be in a 'get your own back' situation.

It was tempting to tackle Peter as an act of retribution, confront him boldly and bludgeon him with all the facts. But I knew my motives should be to achieve justice, awareness-raising and a better life for ADDers and ASSes alike. So much for the theory – let's see what I could do in practice. I made a major effort to keep completely calm, bit the bullet and walked into the dining room.

Chapter 21

A Breakfast Interrupted

"When a thing was new, people said it was not true. Later, when it became obvious, people said it was not important. And when its importance could not be denied, people said it was not new."

(William James, Philosopher, 1842-1910)

Peter, his wife Elizabeth, another woman and three children including Stephen were sitting round a table. Some were buttering or nibbling toast. Others were clutching their warm mugs, elbows resting on the table-top.

"Good morning!" I said, as cheerily as possible, pulling up a chair. Talk about a captive audience. "Would you mind if I joined you for a few minutes?"

"Er, no. Not at all."

They seemed somewhat surprised, but at least they were not objecting.

"I understand that Barney and Lee were being rather disruptive in the lounge last night. I'm sorry if it interfered with your game, or your peace and quiet."

Knowing that Peter had been the principal objector, I looked most intently at him.

"Well, I must admit, I was rather staggered to see a boy of Barney's age playing with toys designed for toddlers. He was darting about all over the place on a plastic lorry, then making the most awful racket with a toy which, I believe, belongs inside a baby's cot," he said.

I paused, and nodded slowly in brief commiseration. "I thought it would be easier for you to understand if I explained to you that Barney has a condition known as Attention Deficit Hyperactivity Disorder – ADHD for short. Do you know anything about it?" Peter looked uncomfortable and shifted on the wooden bench. I was sorry to have to put him through this, but it had to be done.

"Um, well yes. I think I might have heard of it. It's that new thing isn't it?"

"There was a boy in my class who had it, Dad, Bruce Parker!" Stephen piped up.

"Oh really?" I said, turning to Stephen with interest. I had noted Stephen's use of the past tense.

"And is he still in your class?" I added.

"No. He moved to a different school."

I was intrigued.

"Did he now? And which school is that?"

My interest hung on the possibility, however remote, that Bruce had been placed at a school designed for, or at least compatible with, children who have ADHD.

"I don't know." Stephen confessed.

Disappointed, I continued, addressing Peter once more.

"How can I sum up ADHD easily? I once heard an American expert, Dr Sam Goldstein say 'ADHD isn't a problem of knowing what to do but of doing what you know'. I wonder whether you have any idea of the underlying reasons as to why a child with ADHD behaves as he does, and why he finds it so difficult to keep still."

"No, not really." Peter admitted.

As concisely as possible I spoke to the breakfasters about the relative under-functioning of the frontal lobes of the brain, failure to filter incoming stimuli and other neurological aspects. The poor family started to look, inevitably, a little guilty. Trying to show some solidarity I added:

"Misunderstanding a child with ADHD is easily done. I do it myself often with Barney and Adam, and in Barney's case I'm his mother! It's very difficult to remember sometimes, because he looks so normal, that he does have profound neurological differences. If he were a child with Down's Syndrome, for example, you and I would have a constant visual reminder that he is different and we would always be making allowances. The behavioural manifestations of Barney's condition are of the most irritating type, and hard to distinguish from plain naughtiness or disobedience. The commonality of his symptoms – things which any and every child will do from time to time – makes it extremely tricky to handle him fairly."

"It sounds virtually impossible." Peter exclaimed.

"Sometimes it is. Another contributing factor to last night's episode in the lounge was the fact that the effects of Barney's Ritalin had almost certainly worn off by then."

"I've heard about Ritalin. In fact I'm sure I saw an article in a newspaper which called it a 'Zombie Drug'."

Everyone's eyes were upon me now, and I felt accused. I had drugged my child.

I had experienced that same sense of accusation seven years earlier in a different context, when we were living in northern Nigeria for a few months. I was with the children in the market place of Gashua, a medium-sized town, having driven there in our Landrover. Laura was aged seven at the time, and Barney was four. Rear seatbelts were not available in most Nigerian vehicles, so Aaron and I had devised the best system we could to restrain the children when travelling which involved toddlers' harnesses being connected to the chassis. I remember clipping both children into their seats. There was an angry knocking on the window pane.

Although my body was bending over the children, my feet were still outside the vehicle. I stepped back hastily to find out what was the matter. There stood a wizened, elderly Hausa man with most of his front teeth missing. He shouted at me. He waved his hands in the air. He pointed at the children. He scolded me again. He pointed to some passing cattle and screamed some more. I knew very little Hausa but I got the message. He was saying something like "You wicked woman! How could you do such a thing to your children – binding and harnessing them up as if they were animals? Children are meant to run free! Release them immediately!"

How could I begin to explain? I couldn't speak his language except to say 'Hello', 'Goodbye', 'How are you?', 'I am well' and the numbers 1-20. This vocabulary was useless. All I could do was smile, wanly, and drive off.

And now, seven years later, I faced Peter. The difference here was that we spoke the same language. I was in a position to defend myself, and both of us were in a position to debate.

"Ritalin has had very bad press in some quarters," I began, "and I really don't know why. I think it may be tied up with the fact that ADHD itself hasn't yet reached the status of a recognised condition in the public eye. If you are a parent of such a child, you have no doubts. I know many parents whose children have ADHD, and none of them are against Ritalin. I've read of such parents in newspaper articles but I think they form a small minority."

My listeners didn't seem convinced, so I pressed on.

"One article which comes to my mind was about a disillusioned and angry mother of a 14-year-old boy who'd been put on Ritalin three years earlier, when his ADHD was diagnosed. By then, he had severe behavioural problems – violent temper tantrums – and had been excluded from one school after another. Apparently, when he went on Ritalin, she noticed no improvement at all in his behaviour. She even said his tempers were getting worse and that his appetite was suppressed so much that he lost two stone in weight over 10 months."

"That's terrible!" exclaimed one of the women, joining in the conversation.

"It is terrible. But the really terrible thing isn't the drug itself, but the fact that it was still being prescribed and dispensed many months later and no-one seemed to be monitoring, managing or reviewing it."

"It obviously wasn't helping him." said Peter.

"No, it wasn't," I agreed. "Either ADHD was the wrong diagnosis in the first place, or the boy belonged to the 20-30 per cent of ADHD-sufferers who, for some reason, are not helped by the medication. I can't understand why the boy wasn't taken back to the doctor involved for reassessment and why no-one took the boy off Ritalin sooner if he wasn't responding. If the mother was unhappy about it, she could have done that herself. No parent is ever forced to give a child Ritalin.

"Perhaps the paediatrician or child psychiatrist – whoever prescribed the medication – failed to make clear that in the case of a child it is the parents who are in control of the drug and who ultimately decide whether, when and how much Ritalin to give. I don't mean to say that parents have a completely free rein. The maximum amount of Ritalin which the parents could give their child would be limited by the maximum amount which the doctor prescribes. This is around 2.1 milligrammes per kilogramme body-weight of the child, per day, in total, and no single dose of Ritalin should ever exceed 0.6 milligrammes per kilogramme body-weight."

"Are the effects apparent quickly, or do you have to wait days or weeks to see a difference?" asked Peter.

"When you give Ritalin to a child with ADHD, if it works, you soon notice the difference. It takes effect in about 15-20 minutes if the dosage is correct, and once it's kicked in, the child is better able to concentrate. Attention span shoots up and impulsiveness goes down. The fact that the boy in the newspaper article didn't seem to be responding to the Ritalin might even be because the parents were looking at the wrong symptom. Ritalin helps the core symptoms of ADHD – lack of concentration, inattention and impulsiveness – and it often has a beneficial effect on many other problems, such as self-esteem, social skills and oppositionality. Anyway, by itself, Ritalin doesn't stop an angry person being angry. If the boy was angry about the way the adults in his life had treated him, there's no reason to expect that anger to disappear, nor the consequent behavioural problems."

"Well that makes sense, I suppose."

Nodding, I continued. "The real problem might be that he didn't receive Ritalin – and even more importantly, that he hadn't received understanding – early enough in his life for him to be able to modify his own behaviour. If the medication had worked for him he might not have been excluded at all. He might not have had the experiences which led to his anger."

"So do you mean that his mother should have known 15-20 minutes after her boy took his first tablet whether or not it was working?" Elizabeth asked.

"Yes, I do. Though if I'd been her I would have given Ritalin at least a day's trial, probably even a week or more, unless there was a really bad side-effect."

"And to let the child lose two stone! It must have been obvious that something was wrong."

"Any child on Ritalin should be monitored very closely, particularly at the beginning. When Barney was diagnosed with ADHD and prescribed Ritalin, we knew we could stop the medication any time we wanted. Also, he was weighed and measured regularly to make quite sure that he was still growing. He was, and still is."

"So you don't think Ritalin is to blame, then, but rather the mother and the doctors?"

"More the doctors than the mother, that is if we can believe the article in the first place. I don't trust the tabloids to report these stories accurately. If we do assume that the story is true, then the blame lands far more on the doctors. After all, they are meant to be the experts who should be advising the mother. I very much doubt whether she had been ignoring the medical advice, but you never know. What also puzzles me about the article is that I don't think it mentioned any stimulant medications other than Ritalin. If Ritalin fails, a doctor will usually try the child on alternative medication, such as Clonidine or Dextroamphetamine, though these drugs must always be controlled by a professional who understands the complexity of ADHD and the need for careful medical management."

"I take it then that you don't think Ritalin is dangerous, since you're happy for Barney to take it."

"Any drug is dangerous if abused, if taken in overdose, say. Where Ritalin is taken in overdose then it does make the child act robotically and 'zombie'-like. Otherwise, I would say that Ritalin is safe. Extremely safe."

"Has it been well tested, then?"

"Oh yes. There were widespread fears and controversies about the use of Ritalin with children in America from the 1960s to the 1990s. These fears triggered extensive research making it now 'the most well-studied medication in childhood psychiatry'.[38] It's for this reason that I think it is acceptably safe, and also because Barney has been on it for well over three years and he's still alive and kicking. His life and ours have been transformed for the better. I've never heard of anyone dying from taking Ritalin, whereas I've heard of countless deaths from Paracetamol. But people don't go round saying "Ban this terrible drug Paracetamol! Don't give your child Paracetamol!"

"But Ritalin's such a new drug, isn't it? Surely doctors don't know what the long-term effects might be. Isn't that rather scary?"

I wondered whether Peter had heard me when I had spoken about research into the effects of Ritalin going back to the 1960s.

"The use of stimulant medications to treat ADHD isn't particularly new at all. That's one of the myths. Amphetamines, which are stimulants, were used as long ago as 1937 in America, when it was discovered that they reduced disruptive behaviour in certain hyperactive and impulsive children. And methylphenidate hydrochloride (the chemical name for Ritalin) was first used in America in 1957. Not that Ritalin is an amphetamine – it isn't. It's actually classed as a sympathomimetic. Anyway, I can't stress strongly enough that Ritalin is one of the most highly-researched and safest drugs available."

"But it hasn't been around in England that long, has it?"

"No, it hasn't. It was first licensed for use with hyperactivity and made generally available in the late 1980s and early 1990s. Barney first started taking it in 1996."

"But aren't you worried that he'll get addicted?"

"Absolutely not. In fact, there's far more chance of you becoming addicted to that tea and coffee which you're drinking than of Barney becoming addicted to his Ritalin."

They peered down at the hot drinks which they were topping up from time to time.

"In fact caffeine is far, far more addictive than Ritalin, but we don't see health warnings on coffee jars. Ritalin, on the other hand, is a controlled drug and is meant to be kept under lock and key. One of life's little anomalies! As for its addictive properties, I've never yet heard Barney or any child gasp "Give me my Ritalin, quick! I'm dying for another tablet." We often hear people who are desperate for their caffeine dose say "I'm dying for a cuppa." It's precisely because Ritalin is so non-addictive that you can take your child off it quite suddenly, without having to wean him off gradually. It's metabolised completely within about three to four hours. The child never goes through 'cold-turkey' waiting for another tablet. Studies in Massachusetts have shown that if you don't treat adolescents who have ADHD with stimulant medication, they're far more likely to take other, less-desirable drugs. The Americans call it 'SUD' – Substance Use Disorder. Medication for ADHD can reduce SUD in youngsters by 85 per cent".[39]

Peter was not impressed. "But still, despite all that, aren't you worried about any of the side-effects?" he asked.

"In Barney's case, he only has two side-effects that we're aware of, both of them short-lived. One is that he finds it more difficult to go to sleep. The other is a drop in his appetite while the Ritalin is in his system. It is a pain that he doesn't settle as well as he used to at night-time. Also, it can be very annoying when he doesn't want to eat at conventional mealtimes. But he makes up for it most evenings, after his last tablet of the day wears off. He can eat large amounts then. We've learned to adapt to his camel-like eating pattern by now and every time he gets weighed by his paediatrician he has gained weight. We tweak Barney's doses and timings as best we can to keep the side-effects to a minimum and we're absolutely convinced that the benefits of taking Ritalin, in his case, far outweigh any undesirable consequences. We ought to know. We're his parents and we actually live with him."

"Has taking Ritalin helped him a lot, then?"

"Definitely! Before he had medication he was finding life increasingly difficult at school, where demands on his concentration were increasing faster than his ability to cope. His impulsiveness was also causing him to behave in socially unacceptable ways – hitting children, breaking things, using swear words in front of teachers, because he couldn't control his impulsiveness. He became the class scapegoat and was increasingly unacceptable to the other children's parents as a playmate for their child."

"And now?"

"Now he's much better controlled for more of the time. Ritalin gives him a 'window of opportunity' in the classroom during which he is better able to learn in an educational system which isn't ideally planned for him. Life is a lot easier. And Barney's not the only one. Adam is helped by Ritalin too. Another boy in our town, Rory, was into his teens before he was diagnosed with ADHD and prescribed Ritalin. After his very first tablet he said to his mother "Mum, the war in my head has stopped!" I have a friend, Diane, who lives up in the north-east of England. She says her son "didn't have a life" until he was given Ritalin, so extreme was his condition. Most children say that when they're on Ritalin, or some other stimulant medication, they can think more clearly and find it easier to understand what parents and teachers want from them. Their school-work becomes more interesting and enjoyable, their results improve and they make more friends".[40]

"But how does Ritalin work, exactly?"

"It works by stimulating the frontal lobes of the brain and helping the mind to focus. In fact there's a very good analogy to be made with a pair of spectacles; Ritalin focuses the mind just like a pair of spectacles focuses the eyesight. If you have the right prescription for your glasses, you'll at last see clearly. But if your prescription is too strong, you'll still have significant problems seeing. Similarly, if you have the correct prescription for Ritalin, you'll be able to concentrate as well as possible at last, but if your prescription is too strong, you'll over-focus and face an alternative set of problems."

I noticed, for the first time consciously, that Peter was wearing glasses. The lenses caused the sides of his head to appear closer together indicating that he was short-sighted. I chose this as an example.

"Take you and your spectacles, Peter. Imagine that short-sightedness was rare but that you are one of the few people who has it. Imagine that it's so poorly understood that your parents aren't even aware that short-sightedness exists, so it doesn't cross their minds that you have it. You grow from babyhood into childhood and are very shortsighted indeed. You keep banging into things, knocking them over and breaking them. You struggle at school because you can't see the chalkboard and get extremely frustrated. You know, deep inside, that you're different from the other kids and may even be justifiably convinced that you're cleverer than most, but you don't understand how or why you're different. Nobody knows about shortsightedness, so there's no vocabulary to go with this condition, and this further exacerbates the difficulty you have in expressing your problems to anyone. All the time grown-ups are getting at you. 'Peter,' your parents say, 'why on earth do you keep on knocking everything over? Why, oh why do you go on destroying our home? If we've told you once, we've told you a hundred times!' At school it's no better. 'Peter,' your teachers say 'why can't you keep up with the other children? We know you're intelligent. So why do you go on repeatedly failing when we use the chalkboard or overhead projector? Try harder!' You get more and more frustrated. You get detention time and again for failing to complete work in class. Your anger causes you to start misbehaving and you continue to misbehave because you find that it helps to disguise the fact that you're so far behind your peers. You would rather be thought naughty than stupid! Things go from bad to worse as you struggle academically and are seen to fail behaviourally as well. Eventually you are excluded.

"Having undiagnosed ADHD can be just like that. It's possible that the child's parents and teachers don't know that the condition exists. Some people are dismissive, when they hear about it. 'Oh, it's that thing from America', they say. There are even some doctors who don't accept its existence! Kids with ADHD experience problems at home and school similar to those which I've described for a child with undiagnosed eyesight problems."

The whole family continued listening, quietly chewing and sipping from time to time.

"Let's go back to you, Peter, the imaginary child who has severe short-sight which has not been diagnosed. One day, your parents, in desperation, take you to a doctor who happens to be well informed. He tells your parents that there's a condition known as myopia which was first documented nearly a century before in England but has largely gone unrecognised. However, in America, a way of treating this ailment has been invented. Treatment consists of placing onto the bridge of the nose a metal frame containing two circles of glass, kept in place by a pair of metal struts which attach in arcs behind the ears. This treatment isn't without side-effects. Firstly, the weight of the lenses pressing down on the nose causes discomfort. Secondly, there's a danger that the glass might become smashed and cause severe damage to the eye. Thirdly, wearing such a contraption is likely to lead to teasing and taunts from other children. The doctor asks your parents whether, despite these possible side-effects, they would consider the new treatment for their son. What do you think they'd say?"

Peter smiled. He knew exactly where this conversation was leading.

"I know precisely what they'd say because they made such a choice on my behalf many years ago when I was a small boy. I've been wearing glasses ever since," he said.

"And have you regretted it?"

"I regret having to wear glasses at all. But wearing them is much better than leaving them off. I suppose you could say that the benefits out-weigh the drawbacks."

"And that's what I think about Ritalin in relation to Barney. As he grows up into adulthood, in time, he will choose whether to stay on Ritalin or not. And I'm almost certain that he'll make his decision by weighing up the benefits and comparing them to any unpleasant side-effects that he experiences."

"Do adults take Ritalin then?" asked one of the women.

"Some do. I know a man in America who does. He's had ADHD all his life, though it wasn't diagnosed for several decades. He's now in his 40s and takes, I think, five 10-milligramme Ritalin tablets a day. Barney is on three tablets daily, but he has a much smaller body-mass than my American friend. The interesting thing is that there are times when the American chooses to do without his medication – to go 'off meds' as he would say. He's a very creative person and writes brilliant songs. I think it's when he wants to get inspiration for his song-writing that he stops taking the drug. It reminds me of my husband, Aaron, who wears glasses almost all the time but chooses to take them off occasionally when he has to look at things close-up. Being without his glasses in certain situations enables him to work better."

"Fascinating," said Peter.

We must have paused in the conversation because young Stephen actually managed to get a word in edgeways.

"Dad, can I get some more toast? I'm starving!"

Chapter 22

Education, Money and the Criminal Injustice System

∞ *Is not punishment of the offender the defining social glue - and what shall we find to take its place?*

∞ *Should we prescribe drugs which have a likelihood of success and whose effect would save tens of thousands of pounds per criminal per year?*

∞ *Is there a deep sense that somehow treatment 'excuses' criminality, robs us of some need to punish?*

(*A Mind To Crime*, Moir and Jessel, 1995)

One of the great things about the breakfasts served at youth hostels is that nobody goes away hungry. In addition to cereals or fruit juice you can choose to have the full English fry-up and as much toast as you can eat. Stephen was taking advantage of all this as he collected yet another rack-full from the serving hatch.

Elizabeth was looking perturbed.

"What I'm wondering about is all the children with ADHD when they're in the classroom. How do they manage? How do their teachers manage?" she asked.

"With great difficulty," I replied. "School life can become hell – for the kids and their teachers. The teachers are employed to teach children in ways which work best for the majority, that is, those who don't have ADHD. On the whole, this majority do learn, all is well for them and it is rewarding for the teacher too. But when it comes to teaching children with ADHD, and this also applies to kids with dyslexia, the system comes under stress. I'm convinced that we've invented and, during the past three or four decades been continually adapting, an education system which isn't suited to these kids at all. There is so much failure, fear of failure and frustration, that children and staff alike reach breaking point. I've great sympathy for the staff. Almost every one of them, I suspect, entered the teaching profession with the best of motives, eager to impart their wisdom, knowledge and sense of enquiry to young minds. But because they haven't been trained or resourced to teach children with ADHD, what should be a noble pursuit ends up demeaning the teacher and the pupil. As a last resort the teacher can resign – being a teacher isn't compulsory. But the kid can't resign! He might try to do so by playing truant, but he's stuck with compulsory education until he reaches 16, and the school's stuck with him, unless in desperation they end up excluding him."

"So is Barney coping OK in school now that he's on Ritalin?" asked Peter.

"Hmm. A tricky one that. I think the best answer I can give you is 'Yes' and 'No'. Yes, he's coping in that he's no longer the class scapegoat and because staff are more understanding because they know he has an official diagnosis of ADHD, and that I'll be round to the school, immediately, if ever I think he's being discriminated against on account of his ADHD core symptoms. Yes, he's coping in that he's kept on task much better now that he has his medication and a statement of special educational needs which pays for a learning support assistant to give him one-to-one attention for seven hours each week." I paused.

"So what are the 'Nos?" Elizabeth asked.

" No, he's not coping well when he doesn't have his LSA with him. His French and cookery teachers have problems with him. I think it would be possible for his medication to be more 'finely-tuned' so that his concentration is as good as it can be for as long as possible each day. Unfortunately, the staff at Barney's ordinary mainstream school don't have the time or organisational set-up to make this happen. It would involve careful monitoring of Barney's behavioural changes every lesson for a few weeks and matching that pattern with his Ritalin intake in order to get the best schedule possible. We realise that his mainstream school doesn't have the necessary human resources to do this."

"So would you say the answer for Barney and for all children with ADHD is for each of them to have their medication finely-tuned and to have a one-to-one assistant all the time they're in the classroom?"

"Fine-tuning certainly, but as for universal full-time LSAs, no, I don't think that's the answer at all".[41]

"Why not?"

"Many reasons. Firstly, it would be a very inefficient way of running a school. About three per cent of children could have ADHD so we can expect almost every class in a mainstream school to include one such child. They're not rare freaks! Then there are other children with a range of special needs who require assistance. The British Dyslexia Association claim that 10 per cent of children have some degree of dyslexia, and about four per cent are severely affected. If every child with ADHD, ADD and dyslexia had a personal assistant, then school would be an extremely labour-intensive system.

"Secondly, the presence of an LSA draws attention to the child's condition, and singles him out as different. This support system was invented, I think, to keep as many children as possible in mainstream schools – to serve the god called 'inclusion'. It is politically correct to try and keep every sort of child in their local school. There are disadvantages for children who feel inadequate alongside other children with greater ability. Barney has frequently destroyed his work because it did not stand up to comparison with the achievements of his peers."

"And thirdly?" Elizabeth suggested.

"Thirdly, there is the gender issue. Most kids with ADHD are boys. Almost all LSAs are women. There is a shortage of men in primary education and the absence of enough good male role models is intensified for children who spend most of their time supported in all their work by a woman. Being attached to a female assistant is seen as 'uncool'. Barney's SENCO told us that by the time boys are at secondary school, many of them would rather fail than be seen to be chaperoned by a woman."

"I can believe that," said Peter, sympathetically.

"Then fourthly, there's the whole question of expertise. The rate of pay for most LSAs is appallingly low. Often they are mothers who want a job which ties in with school hours. This doesn't mean they do a bad job – far from it. It is important that provision is made for in-service training so that complex conditions like ADHD, ADD and dyslexia can be better understood. Many undergo further training but the more qualified they become, the more likely they are to leave for better-paid work. Lack of continuity makes it hard for the child. Some of the best LSAs are those who do it year in, year out, as a labour of love."

"Bruce has dyslexia as well as ADHD," chipped in Stephen.

"Many children do," I said, affirming Stephen's comment. "Fifthly and sixthly, there are the matters of curriculum and the teaching methods which are employed. We're convinced that Barney and many other children like him need a specialised curriculum. Barney needs more of the things in which he can succeed, such as sports and percussion, art and other practical subjects. An LSA isn't trained or employed to deliver radically alternative teaching techniques which make it easier for the kid to learn. Unfortunately, she and the teacher just go on delivering the standard education which fails for these children's neurological differences. The poor kids get pushed and pushed to become more like the other youngsters in the class. You can't just use run-of-the-mill remedial methods to help children with ADHD - you have to use proper neuro-education."

"Neuro-education?"

"Yes, neuro-education. To quote someone called William Cruickshank, one of the few people who really understands the needs of these kids:

"Remediation techniques are not satisfactory with children with learning disabilities when these learning deficits are the result of a diagnosed or presumed neuro-physiological dysfunction." [42]

"You obviously don't think much of LSAs then," said Elizabeth.

"It's the system that I don't think much of. My verdict on LSAs is that they work very hard and are the unsung heroines (and very occasional hero) of the school. Those who stick it out with a kid who has ADHD are particularly heroic. I met one LSA who admitted to me that assisting a child with ADHD had been the least satisfying of all the posts she had ever held. Apparently, she felt as if she was hitting her head against a brick wall a lot of the time when the boy couldn't keep on task. LSAs probably do a great job with many of the children who are just slow-learners but when it comes to assisting kids with ADHD, ADD and dyslexia they're simply, through no fault of their own, the wrong type of 'animal'. I must stress though that most of what I'm saying is based mainly on my experience with Barney. A sample of one is hardly significant, but I'm fairly convinced that most of the arguments do apply more generally."

"What do you mean by the 'wrong type of animal'?" asked Peter.

"Well, in Barney's situation – meaning no disrespect to either of them – putting his LSA with him is like pairing a mature female anteater with a young male parrot, in a school designed for anteaters. It should be obvious that instead of attaching this anteater to that parrot in order to get him to learn like an anteater, it would make more sense to send him to a school designed for parrots. If inclusion is an absolute necessity, then there must be parrot-friendly teaching methods and a parrot-friendly curriculum in place. It's cruel and pointless to try and force the parrot to become an anteater." In the case of ADHD the problems faced by the parrot are compounded out of all proportion because the parrot looks exactly like an anteater.

"So, what on earth do you suggest can be done for children with ADHD then?" asked Peter.

"That is the $64,000 question – or maybe that's been superseded by the $1,000,000 question!" I replied.

"I'm not an expert in education, so I can't answer that with any authority. The best I can do is observe and analyse what's going wrong for Barney and others like him. I can only really guess at possible solutions. There's plenty of evidence to suggest that an ADHD-friendly educational model would be far more experience-based than the one we have at present. When the children do, inevitably, have to tackle the three 'R's, they'd certainly benefit from smaller class sizes, the minimum number of classroom changes, distraction-free zones and information presented for 20 to 30 minutes, with an activity break every 40 to 45 minutes. There is also a need for more frequent PE lessons for the particularly active kids.

"Paul Cooper and Katherine Ideus at Cambridge University suggest many other effective teaching methods too.[43] It can also help if kids with ADHD have far greater access to computers to relieve the stress of having to do so much handwriting."

"I find all that rather difficult to imagine in a situation of inclusion within the classroom," said Elizabeth. "You either run the whole thing round the kids with ADHD or you don't. I can't conceive of any middle way."

"Neither can I," I agreed. "Maybe inclusion can only work if the whole thing does revolve around the children who have ADHD. I know that when I run a programme for the Beaver Scouts, if I've designed it with ADHD in mind, it also works very well for all the kids, regardless of their neurology. But what we really need, I think, is for our schools, LEAs and government to learn from people who are experts in this area. There are some in this country, as well as Cooper and Ideus. There are a few schools, independent ones, where children with ADHD are being appropriately educated. There are other countries way ahead of ours."

"Such as?"

"America and Australia – and Finland too where, I believe, they screen children for ADHD before they start school. We've got so much to learn. But it's not impossible."

"Well, it's pretty obvious what's stopping such progress," Peter interjected.

"Is it? What?" I asked.

"Money, of course. It always boils down to money in the end," he said.

"I expect you're right, but getting ADHD sorted out as early as possible, and in particular giving children an ADHD-friendly education, would almost certainly pay for itself in the end. The case for early diagnosis and treatment as opposed to ignoring the condition is overwhelming. Getting ADHD diagnosed by a qualified professional costs around £500. A year's supply of Ritalin tablets is about £200. A statement of special educational needs at Level G, which is what Barney has, provides £2,330 each year to the school. Add that up and call it about £3,000 a year. In contrast, the potential cost of not diagnosing and treating someone with ADHD could mean the cost of imprisoning them. That's about £26,000 a year, rising to £62,400 for someone placed in a high security unit [44]."

"Prison! That sounds alarming." Peter said.

"It is. But the statistics are there. They indicate that most children who are excluded or in pupil referral units or on remand, and adults in jail have ADHD, ADD and/or dyslexia. Prevention is far better than cure."

"Have you spoken to David Blunkett, the Minister for Education, about any of this?" Elizabeth asked, though whether it was with tongue in cheek I could not tell.

"I have written to him, yes. I think the whole government, not just the ministers of education, need to take ADHD very seriously indeed. Its implications are so great. I would even call it a burning issue of our time. And if they're not already convinced, then I think they're under obligation to investigate the matter and let the facts speak for themselves. The social consequences of undiagnosed and unaddressed ADHD must be identified, and health, education, and social services' policy modified accordingly. A friend of mine in the USA who works in the criminal justice system and knows a lot about ADHD says that over there the government is being forced to consider new approaches. Their jails are full and the cost of building more is prohibitive."

"So are you saying that there's a direct link between having ADHD and criminality, then?" Peter looked fairly aghast.

"What I am saying is that if someone has ADHD they are far more likely to end up in trouble with the law than if they don't have ADHD. Someone with ADHD is impulsive and frequently fails to think of the consequences of their actions – it's easy to see how they land themselves in trouble. I've heard a story about a teenager with ADHD who was arrested following an armed robbery. He'd been persuaded by the leader of the gang (who probably didn't have ADHD) to hold the gun during the raid. He hadn't even known that there was going to be a robbery until a few minutes before it happened. He was taken advantage of by the others who used him."

"Or abused him," Peter corrected me.

"Quite. It went from bad to worse. When he was interviewed he got the sequence of events mixed up because of his problems with understanding the time, and started contradicting himself. When he got into the courtroom he was so distracted by everyone and everything around him that he failed to keep his eye on the judge and was accused of having a bad attitude in the courtroom."

"Did the authorities know that he had ADHD?" Peter asked.

"I don't know, that's the trouble with stories. But the point is, the core symptoms of ADHD counted against him all through the so called 'justice' procedure and much of the evidence was wrongly interpreted as a result. He was sentenced far more harshly than he would have been had his condition been properly understood and taken into account. Very few prisoners are ever treated for ADHD while they're in jail. Even if they have a diagnosis they are frequently forbidden access to their medication. The situation is scandalous. Without medication and other forms of appropriate treatment their time spent in prison is fruitless. When they come out it's rare for their families to let them come back home and many re-offend. It is usual for prisoners to be released with their possessions and a sum of money . Anyone with ADHD is likely to spend the whole amount within the first few hours of release, with no thought to the future or expedient spending whatsoever."

"But what do you think can be done about it?" asked Elizabeth.

"That's a huge question, and I'd never pretend to have all the answers. But for a start, members of the legal profession and the police should be educated about ADHD. When suspects are questioned in custody, it should always be on the interrogator's mind that the subject might have ADHD. Interviewing techniques should be structured to help the suspect put events into the correct sequence."

"You mean like asking 'What happened first?', and 'What happened next?' and so on?"

"Yes. Precisely. And it must be understood that some kids with ADHD don't grasp the seriousness of the situation at all. Their limited attention span means that they can't cope with long sessions – either under interrogation or in the courtroom. Sometimes they impulsively confess to a crime which they didn't commit simply to make the interrogator stop."

"It sounds to me as though 'justice' is not really being done." Peter pointed out.

"It isn't. Unless and until everyone understands ADHD and takes it into account, the term 'justice' is a misnomer. Sometimes I wonder if we live in a society which wants to see people punished rather than helped. We have a 'Criminal Injustice System'. When there's a general election, I'll be voting for the first political party to have become ADHD-aware and whose manifesto shows solid evidence of this."

The hostel warden entered the dining room, ready to clear away the used cutlery and crockery of breakfasters who had finished long ago. We rose hastily. Peter, Elizabeth and their entourage stacked their cups, bowls and plates as quickly as possible.

"I'd better get ready myself," I said as I left the table.

Excusing myself with a smile and a wave, I sidled out of the room and made my escape.

Chapter 23

Philosophy in the Washroom

"One of the annoying things about believing in free will and individual responsibility is the difficulty of finding somebody to blame your problems on. And when you do find somebody, it's remarkable how often his picture turns up on your driver's licence." §

(P.J. O'Rourke)

I glanced into the lounge and saw the boys amusing themselves with a boxed game.

"Did you tell him, Mum?" Barney asked, eager to know the answer.

"Yes, Barney. It would be quite accurate to say that I did. He has, in no uncertain terms, been told."

That was all Barney wanted to know. He immediately dropped the matter and returned his attention to the game. He was being, for the while at least, what society terms 'a good boy'. I smiled and went upstairs to the dormitory.

It was a complete tip. Clothes, sleeping bags, torches and toothbrushes were scattered all over the place. I sighed, picked up my wash-kit and towel, and walked down one flight of stairs to the ladies' washrooms. Choosing one from the row of washbasins I put the plug in and turned on the tap. The water ran clear and warm and I remembered my early hostelling days, decades before, when many of the hostels did not provide hot water. Standards had definitely risen over the years.

When I had almost finished, Elizabeth came in, looking for her hand-towel and soap. We greeted each other again.

"That was very interesting – what you had to say about ADHD, I mean," she commented.

"I hope you found it helpful, and will do in the future, too." I pulled the plug out of the sink. The water made a rude noise as it gurgled away.

"One thing I was wondering," she ventured, "was whether there's any test[45] you can do to prove for certain whether a child has ADHD or not?"

"Well, the answer to that isn't completely straightforward. There are some tests you can do in which radioactive glucose is administered to the person who may have ADHD and then the way in which it is metabolised can be picked up on a device called a PET scanner. 'PET' stands for 'Positron Emission Tomography'. However, it is very expensive, not readily available and unacceptable to do this test on children because of the substances involved. I think there are also laboratory tests which can be done to measure dopamine uptake in the brain. Then there are push-button tests which pick up just how much trouble a boy has in refraining from pressing a button that he's not supposed to press. The blood flow inside the brain can also be imaged at the same time using functional magnetic resonance imaging – fMRI for short. Imaging can be carried out before and after administering Ritalin. It seems that boys with ADHD not only improve their task performance a lot after taking medication, but also this improvement corresponds with increased blood flow to certain parts of the brain.[46] I don't know if they've done any tests on girls yet."

"Oh? Why's that then?"

"Probably because there are so many more hyperactive and impulsive boys than there are girls."

"Aren't there any tests which can be done somewhere other than in a hospital or a laboratory?"

"Well, there's something called the Conners' Continuous Performance Test which is normally given by an educational psychologist, but could be used by any intelligent person who has access to the computer programme. You can administer it to anyone over about six years of age and it takes 14 minutes to complete. The sorts of things which it measures include things like risk-taking, reaction time, omission and commission errors. Strictly speaking, you can't use this test alone to diagnose ADHD, because other medical conditions could produce similar results."

"Such as?"

"Such as an anxiety disorder or post-traumatic stress disorder perhaps[#]. So ADHD must first be diagnosed by some other means. Then the Conners test can be very useful in plotting changes in a particular individual's attention span and impulsivity over time, or in a variety of situations. You can buy the relevant CD or disk for around £300."

"Not particularly cheap, is it?"

"No, but another form of assessment is cheaper and is also the most universally accepted method at the moment."

"What's that?"

"Well it isn't really a test at all – just how closely the ADHD-suspect measures up to a list of criteria defined by the American Psychiatric Association. They call it the DSM-IV for short and it stands for 'The Diagnostic and Statistical Manual of Mental Disorders, Fourth Edition – Diagnostic Criteria for Attention Deficit/Hyperactivity Disorder (AD/HD)".[47]

"So presumably Barney fits the criteria?"

"He does, and he was showing the signs and symptoms before he was seven years old, which in itself is one of the criteria."

"If that's so, then what you're saying implies that if you don't have ADHD before the age of seven then you can't ever have it."

"Yes, it does imply exactly that. The problem is that doctors are coming across more and more impulsive and inattentive young people who are older than seven, and adults too, who simply don't remember having had symptoms of ADHD when they were younger than seven. Their parents and friends say the same. This poses a huge problem when such people are now turning up with enough of the other criteria which do satisfy a diagnosis of ADHD."

"So you mean that they can't actually be diagnosed."

"More or less. And all because of Criterion 'B' in the DSM-IV. I've heard, on the grapevine, that there are moves afoot to get this criterion removed so that people with so-called 'Late Onset ADHD' can get the help they need."

"There's a lot involved with ADHD, that's for sure," said Elizabeth, "but one thing in particular has been bothering me a lot in all this."

Elizabeth appeared hesitant to spit it out – almost too frightened and apologetic to ask. I had the distinct impression that the imminent question was really what she was most interested in and, had we not just had all the preamble about ADHD testing, she would not have had the courage to dare make her next enquiry.

"Please do ask – I don't mind," I tried to encourage her.

"Well, it's about Ritalin and how it interferes with the child's mind. If it interferes with his behaviour, then isn't it interfering with his free will? Aren't you changing his basic personality, and has anyone got the right to do that to somebody else?"

"That is a very good question," I replied, trying to be reassuring, "and one which I agonised over myself before we agreed for Barney to go on Ritalin."

I paused, wondering where to begin, drew breath and then continued.

"It's not a straightforward question to answer though because, strictly speaking, one ought to establish whether such a thing as 'free will' exists or not in the first place. The whole matter of free will has occupied the mind of philosophers and theologians for centuries – if not for millennia. I don't think it's possible to prove whether or not free will exists. But you ought to be able to give good reasons as to why you think it does, or doesn't, exist."

Elizabeth nodded, so I continued.

"For myself, I'm convinced that it has to exist in some shape or form. If we don't have free will, then we're not capable of making any real choices at all, including moral choices. As part of my Christian faith I believe in the reality of selfishness, obedience, disobedience, responsibility, choices, judgment and, above all, in the reality of love. The whole concept of judgment, for example, would be nonsensical if we had no free will. Jesus didn't mince his words when he criticised the Pharisees for being hypocrites. If they'd had no choice in their attitudes or words, the whole idea of hypocrisy would be meaningless too. As for love, well what would love mean if we're mere robots with our behaviour deterministically pre-programmed? Jesus said 'If you love me, you will keep my commandments'.[48] There's no room for determinism here!"

"But surely Christians aren't the only ones who believe in free will?" said Elizabeth, perhaps by way of an objection.

"By no means. Anyone who ever complains about someone else's behaviour, or who blames another person, believes in free will. It's a give-away."

"Well, I don't know anybody who doesn't fall into that category," Elizabeth pointed out.

"Neither do I. Our experience is that virtually everyone does believe in free will, even if they claim not to. The great 18th Century philosopher Immanuel Kant called this belief in man's free will a practical postulate – something which can't be proved, but for practical purposes must be assumed. That is a useful idea to consider if we want to think about how free our free will is."

"And just how free do you think it is?"

"Free enough! But if Kant was right we may not be exercising the freedom as often as we think. Kant maintained that we only exercise our free will when we make a moral choice and do what we know to be right in a situation, in other words, obey our conscience, regardless of whether it's comfortable or convenient for us. If you go around doing whatever you feel like, you're not especially free. It could be argued that you've used your freedom to silence the voice of conscience, but the result is that in some sense you will dehumanise yourself because you simply end up following your animal instincts. St Paul, who as well as being an Apostle was a brilliant theologian, explained the loss of true freedom and independence which accompanies selfishness as 'becoming a slave of sin'.[49] Actually, he was quoting Jesus' own words when he said 'Truly truly, I say to you, every one who commits sin is a slave to sin'".[50]

"Yes, but how does all this relate to ADHD?" Elizabeth pulled me back to our discussion.

"It is relevant. Let's suppose that Jesus, St Paul and Immanuel Kant have given us a good description of the human condition. If, then, we want to observe another human being acting in a way that is most free, we can observe this when we see them doing something which is kind, noble and courageous, in a situation where it is against their own personal interests. They've chosen freely to act in accordance with the moral law inside them, despite their self-centred, 'animal' desires to either run away or go-with-the-flow – whatever would come naturally, easily and most pleasantly.

If I consider times I have seen Barney acting like that, and ask myself whether, at such times he's been on or off Ritalin, the answer, undoubtedly, is when he is ON Ritalin. He has more frequently been able to behave in a kind, thoughtful and altruistic manner when he's taken his medication. Ritalin has enabled him to focus so that his impulsiveness is kept under sufficient control, enabling him to make the choices which, deep down, he wanted to make all along – choices that you or I could have made far more easily because of our advantages of lower distractibility and greater self-regulation."

Elizabeth looked very thoughtful.

“What I’m saying is that Ritalin doesn’t diminish the free will of a child – or adult – with ADHD. On the contrary, it actually enhances it. Perhaps it would be more accurate to say that it enhances the capacity of a person with ADHD to exercise their free will. I don’t believe that applying medication to the human brain can ever raise it above its potential. Imagine giving a Ritalin tablet to a cauliflower. It won’t transform it into either a genius or a saint because the potential for either of those things isn’t present in the cauliflower in the first place! Ritalin can only help someone reach their potential. If it doesn’t do that, then there is no point in taking it.”

Elizabeth laughed. “Well, that’s quite a claim for a mere chemical tablet!”

“I suppose it is. If it’s accurately prescribed, wisely used and always given and received with consent (Barney, incidentally, accepts his tablets very happily), my verdict is that Ritalin, far from morally degrading and damaging a person with ADHD, can, under certain circumstances, enhance their humanity. I haven’t got shares in any company which manufactures the stuff. I’m just profoundly grateful for the positive changes which my son has experienced since he started the medication.”

Chapter 24

A Population Explosion of Adders?

Socrates: *Do you know what the best contraceptive is?*

Plato: *No.*

Socrates: *Precisely. Your answer is correct, my friend.*

Elizabeth was now well stuck into our conversation. Something further appeared to cross her mind and, sensing this, I propped myself on the edge of one of the basins and waited.

"You know there's something else about all this which puzzles me," she began.

"And what's that?"

"Well, I know that five years ago, say, and the whole of my life before that, I'd definitely never heard about ADHD at all. I'm pretty sure now that I have heard about it a few times, and quite recently when Stephen told me about his friend Bruce. It's clear from all that you've been saying that ADHD has been around a long time. But is it suddenly becoming more common or something? Is the reason why it's getting to be more of an issue is because more children are born with it? Or is it just as prevalent as it always was, but because of better publicity more people know about it?"

"I think the answer is both. Yes, there is a much greater awareness of it now than there used to be, and yes, I believe that there are good reasons to think that ADHD is becoming more common. I've never heard anyone else say this and there may not be any evidence to prove it."

"So why do you think it is that ADHD is getting so much more publicity than it used to, then?"

"I think it's partly because our world is becoming more and more complicated. Dr Sam Goldstein, in America, says that the more complex a society is, the more premium we put on self-control."

"Yes. I think the world is more complicated. When I think back to my childhood and how our family, time and money were organised and then compare it to our family today I can see how much more, well, more elaborately we live now! Things just aren't as simple now as they used to be."

"No, they aren't," I agreed. "But I think that the main reason why ADHD is getting more publicity now can be summed up in Tony Blair's famous three words – 'Education! Education! Education!' There are lots of difficulties for parents of children with ADHD but the biggest problem for us all is education. We agonise over getting the right kind of schooling for Barney. We know that mainstream schooling is inappropriate, but it's so difficult to get anything done about it. This country used to have different sorts of schools for different sorts of children but now, because of the policy of inclusion, all children have to fit into one sort of school. A pioneering headmaster at the end of the 19th Century, F. W. Sanderson, was described by H. G. Wells as 'The Great Schoolmaster'. Sanderson's theme was 'Education must be fitted to the boy; not the boy to education'.[51] If only Barney's educators were taking that attitude. All our problems would be solved."

"But surely special schools still exist," protested Elizabeth.

"Yes, that's true. But I'm thinking primarily of children with ADHD. For a child to be sent by a local education authority to a special school, either he or she has to have very profound visible special needs which can't be ignored without the general population protesting on behalf of the child." I paused.

"Or?" Elizabeth prompted.

"Or the child has to have a very marked and easily measurable difference – IQ for example. In our county, we've been told that only children whose IQ falls below about 68 qualify for entry to an MLD Special School. 'MLD' stands for Moderate Learning Difficulties. Kids like Barney and Adam, who are fairly typical of children with ADHD, in general don't qualify for special education on either count. Although there is a test which can be used to get an objective measurement of their impulsiveness and concentration problems, the educational psychologist at our LEA cannot or will not administer it. We've asked that Barney be investigated using this method, but we were told that they 'don't use this test'. Also we were told that the test was unnecessary since Barney's ADHD was not in dispute – they had accepted the diagnosis from the paediatrician...But I think they missed the point completely. The reason that we want a measurement of this aspect of Barney's difficulties is so that we have some objective data which indicates the degree of his problem. This might be very important if ever the LEA threaten to withdraw his Statement of Special Educational Needs."

"So what you're saying is that although children with ADHD need special education, they can't get it because they look too normal and the LEA's educational psychologists refuse to measure these kids' most relevant difficulties," concluded Elizabeth.

"Yes. If teaching techniques could be used so that Barney could be included and have his needs met, then we'd be perfectly happy. But that isn't the case. Our experience is based in one school but I have met many parents of children with ADHD from all over the country and it looks as though the situation is very much the same throughout England and Wales."

"This does sound like a sorry state of affairs."

"It is. I've only heard of one real success story, and that's about a boy who lives in a village in the north-west of England. He goes to his local comprehensive school which only has 180 pupils and a strong special needs department. What's more, he had the good fortune to have a very dedicated head teacher and staff at his primary school. They worked very hard with him and for him, through very difficult times, and didn't give up. Mainly I hear that the education of most children with ADHD in mainstream schools is a series of disasters."

"Don't children who have ADHD ever go to special schools then?"

"Yes, sometimes they do. Some children end up going to a special school because the teachers in the mainstream school can't handle their behaviour. Often these kids have been excluded from their local school before they end up in a school or special unit for the 'EBDs'."

"EBDs? What are they?"

"EBD stands for children with Emotional and Behavioural Difficulties. I'm convinced the reason why most of these kids have become EBD, is because their ADHD has been undiagnosed, misunderstood and ignored when they were younger. What's more, their core symptoms have been exacerbated by the school environment in which they have been trapped from the age of five."

Elizabeth looked justifiably troubled. "That's terrible, and so unnecessary."

"It is. They're initially included in mainstream schools because the government decides to give all students the opportunity to learn to value diversity and develop natural friendships in their home communities. Great in theory! But in practice, if they fail to take proper account of these kids' neurological differences, both kids and teachers suffer. No wonder so many teachers are stressed-out and so many are leaving the profession."

"True," Elizabeth concurred, "I can name at least two friends who fall into that category."

"So can I. And how many teachers, with the best will in the world, have the time to differentiate their teaching every single lesson for the children who have ADHD, in addition to the dyslexics and other special-needs kids?" I asked.

"Do you think there's a child with ADHD in every class then?" asked Elizabeth.

"More or less, yes. Roughly three per cent of children have ADHD, which means in a class of 30 kids you can expect one such child. So the government is right that every teacher has to be a special needs teacher, but I don't think this is either realistic or reasonable. I think that teaching kids with special educational needs is very different from teaching kids who are academically gifted and who learn easily by conventional methods. Why should all teachers have to be all things to all kids? Every teacher is unique with a unique set of gifts and preferences. There must be thousands of teachers who went into teaching because they loved their special subject, with no thought that they would be involved with special-needs children."

"I'm sure that was true of my teachers, when I was at school," Elizabeth said, nodding.

"Mine too. But while these teachers have been in the profession, the ideology of 'inclusion' has grown. There are fewer special schools and it must seem from these teachers' perspective that special-needs kids have been smuggled into their classrooms through the back door. Teachers who are being trained now are supposed to be made aware that their work will include working with children with special-needs. I think this policy deters many talented people from going into the profession. I know it certainly puts me off, not that I'm claiming to be talented. I just don't have the patience to make a special needs teacher."

"I can't say that I'd have enough patience either."

"I think it makes far more sense and is far less stressful for pupils and staff alike if the various types of needs and personalities can be better matched. I've nothing against inclusion. I think it sounds wonderful, in principle, and I know that the benefits for some children, say those confined to wheelchairs, can be enormous."

"I suppose their peers profit too by learning to accept people with disabilities. I guess they have the chance to befriend them."

"Yes, maybe they do, but many kids with ADHD do not have a positive experience of inclusion, probably because their disability is neurological and invisible."

"Yes. Your Barney certainly looks quite normal."

"Everyone can see that a child in a wheelchair needs certain special arrangements, and these can be provided where there's the good will to make inclusion work. Including kids with ADHD can only work if the staff and pupils are well informed about ADHD. But it's such a complex condition."

"All the pupils, as well as staff? That's rather a tall order, isn't it?"

"It is. But otherwise children with ADHD will be misunderstood and inappropriately treated by the teachers and the children. We don't care what system is used to educate Barney, as long as it works. We don't want him continually excluded from activities which demand that he has the right equipment in the right place at the right time, because he is bound to be disorganised. As things stand in mainstream schooling there's not enough pastoral support. Right now, Barney's stuck in a school where the evidence points to only a small proportion of staff having a real heart for teaching kids with problems like his."

"It seems to me, then, that many needy children, particularly those with ADHD, are being left high and dry." said Elizabeth.

"I think they are." I agreed with her. "Over the years, the diversity of our schools has decreased and kids with ADHD have been channelled into less suitable schools. At the same time, the curriculum has also become more academic and all these factors combine to make the ADHD kids like square pegs forced into increasingly rounded holes. No wonder they're more noticeable, diagnoses have risen and there's more publicity."

"But if ADHD isn't 'new' - if it's been around for centuries and centuries, why don't we hear of historical figures who had it?" asked Elizabeth.

"Oh, but we do - if you read the right books! Benjamin Franklin in the 18th century, Thomas Edison in the 19th and Ernest Hemingway in the 20th century all undoubtedly had ADHD.[52] It wasn't called ADHD, of course, in their days. In fact it wasn't really called anything at all except perhaps 'Minimal Brain Dysfunction' by the time Hemingway reached his later years. But you know, there are two sets of facts which, when you put one alongside the other, point to a fascinating possible link between education and the public perception of ADHD."

"So, what are they then?"

"Well, the first set of facts is about the introduction of compulsory education in England. Apparently, although there was a famous Education Act of 1870 which empowered School Boards to make by-laws compelling children to attend school, compulsory education only spread gradually. Many districts weren't covered by School Boards and were served only by voluntary schools.[53] A bit later on, additional education acts in 1876 and 1880 finally made school attendance compulsory for all children.[54] But it wasn't until 1899 when the National Board of Education was established that free public education was available to all kids in England.[55] By that year, the minimum leaving age had been raised to 12, although 11 years was still accepted after that in certain rural communities. And it was just three years later, in 1902, that School Boards were abolished and replaced by Local Education Authorities, one of their responsibilities being the building of new council secondary grammar schools. So public secondary education became available as well. That's the first fact.

The second is that the first medical researcher into ADHD, a paediatrician called George Still, described the condition in a series of 20 lectures to the Royal College of Physicians in 1902. He also had a paper published that year in *The Lancet*. The question is, can this be just coincidence? Doesn't it strike you, Elizabeth, as being possible that these two events are connected? It's been estimated that the proportion of the labouring classes' children which attended school (mostly Sunday schools) in the first few years of Victoria's reign was somewhere between one-third and one-half.[56] This proportion rose during the course of her reign. By the 1880s, inspectors in London were doing a thorough job seeking out the homeless 'street Arabs' who lived in railway arches and in places such as the cellars of unfinished houses – some half-a-million of them.[57]

"Good grief!" interrupted Elizabeth "I never realised that there were as many homeless youngsters as that!"

"It's shocking, isn't it? But I suspect that many of these children had ADHD. After all, like today, these kids are found in disproportionately high numbers in situations where family protection and care has broken down. The only difference today is that we have social services, children's homes, fostering and adoption schemes.

"When Queen Victoria died in 1901, virtually all children up to the age of 12 were in school. Before that, if there was a child with ADHD who had actually been sent to school but didn't 'get on', he wouldn't be forced to attend."

"No, I suppose he wouldn't."

"What's more, if his parents had to pay school fees, they'd be reluctant to continue spending money on education for a kid who was clearly better off doing interesting things elsewhere. Once law and practice conspired to put all children into school at the turn of the century, we have a unique moment in our history. For the first time ever, children with ADHD are compelled to spend a vast proportion of their childhood cooped up in a restrictive, ADHD-hostile, environment. The result? Possibly that it propagated the first generation of children in which a type emerged - that type which George Still described as 'aggressive, defiant and resistant to discipline'. I think it's a reasonable hypothesis."

Elizabeth opened her mouth to reply but was interrupted by an impatient knocking on the washroom door.

"There you are," said Peter, looking somewhat exasperated. "We're all waiting for you you know."

Elizabeth glanced at her watch. "Oops!" she exclaimed, "I've got to go. Nice to chat, and all the best with Barney."

"Thanks." I replied.

∞ ∞ ∞

Elizabeth's interest and prompting questions had helped me to clarify my thoughts and I wanted to complete this process by considering my ideas about why ADHD is on the increase in absolute terms. I was alone and it was quiet so I could take a few more precious minutes to think things over.

The history of research in this field is short but there are enough fairly well-established facts about the procreative activities of both ADDers and ASSes to justify an educated guess about future population trends. Consider the following points and deductions:

1. ASSes find it far easier than ADDers to organise themselves, to think before they act and to consider the future consequences of their actions.
2. Reliable contraception has only been easily available in our country for, say, the last 50 to 100 years.
3. In order for contraception to be used effectively, those who use it must be able to organise themselves, have good control over the impulsive side of their nature and have the ability to think ahead.
4. It is therefore reasonable to conclude that ASSes will tend to make much more effective use of contraception than ADDers.
5. Those who use contraceptives effectively tend to limit the number of children they produce or to have no children at all.
6. Russell Barkley, American ADHD expert, has data which indicate that among males up to 20 years of age, 41 times as many babies are sired by ADDers compared to ASSes.

7. Because of significant genetic factors (ADHD is highly heritable), on the whole ADDers beget ADDers while ASSes beget ASSes.

8. Well-organised ASSes, men and women, are, for a variety of reasons, choosing to wait some years before starting a family.

9. Consider the following statement by Cooper and Ideus from the University of Cambridge:

   "Most girls with AD/HD struggle silently, ignored by teachers and peers, falling behind socially and academically. In adolescence, they have poor self-esteem, accrued over the years, and may turn to substance abuse and sexual promiscuity in an effort to gain peer acceptance" [58].

10. ADDers, therefore, are reproducing themselves in greater numbers, and at an earlier age.

So what could this mean in practical terms? It means that as time goes on, the percentage of ADDers in the general population will increase, while that of ASSes will decrease. Since it is more difficult for ADDers than ASSes to maintain stable family relationships, the proportion of children with ADHD who are in care or placed for adoption will continue to increase. Already it has been estimated that up to 20 per cent of children who are adopted have ADHD.[59]

Very similar arguments have been used for social groups that are regarded as 'undesirable'. The Nazis used them about the Jews; Protestants about Catholics; English about the Irish; Brits about foreign immigrants; middle-class people about the working class; and people with high IQs about people with low IQs. The arguments about differential procreation rates are matters of debate and controversy, and on the whole such scaremongering has proved to be exaggerated . The last thing that I want to do is stigmatise ADHD as a 'threat' which is going to take over the population. But I do want to emphasise that there are good reasons for thinking that the number of people who have ADHD in our population is on the increase.

If this is so then, unless major changes are made in our schools, teachers and pupils will come under increasing stress and our education system will be unable to educate all our young people.

Chapter 25

Horns or Thorns?

"...a thorn was given me in the flesh...Three times I besought the Lord about this, that it should leave me, but he said to me 'My grace is sufficient for you, for my power is made perfect in weakness.'"

(St Paul, Apostle and Theologian, 2 Corinthians 12:7, 8)

"There is no gathering of the rose without being pricked by the thorns." §

(Pilpay {or Bidpai}, *The Two Travellers*, Chapter ii. Fable vi.)

When I returned to the dormitory an astonishing sight awaited me. Gone were our clothes; vanished our rucksacks; spotless the room. This could have indicated a theft. The more likely alternative was that Super-Aaron had arrived. There is no-one else who has a greater capacity for putting into reverse the Second Law of Thermodynamics...I don't know anyone else who can clear up messes so swiftly or so well. He burst into the room. All of a sudden he was there, in front of me.

"Aaron!"

"Anna!"

We embraced.

"Where have you been?" he asked.

"In the loo," I replied.

It was clear that since I had been absent so long he was wondering which particular bowel condition was ailing me but he did not ask.

"Come on," he said, "the boys and luggage are in the car, waiting! We've got no time to lose. Adam's got to be at his football match at 10.15 and we've got to be in church by 10.45."

"Well, if you've packed everything, I'm ready. Oh – have you cleared our stuff out of the drying room?"

"Yeah, yeah!" he replied.

We made our way outside to the car park. I remembered that I had not asked the warden if there was a duty we could do. But it was too late to ask now. I salved my conscience by reminding myself that between us Aaron and I had cleared and cleaned up after our trails of destruction, and most of the time these days that was all the warden would ask.

It was easy to spot our car. It was the one bouncing up and down. Barney, Adam and Lee, although strapped in the back, were by no means motionless.

"So, did you have a good time?" Aaron asked me as I fastened my seatbelt.

"Did we? You bet! It was brilliant! I can't believe so much has happened in less than a day."

The memory of a host of people and events flooded through my mind: our fellow passengers on the trains; the Bellowing Killjoy; Jenny Newbold and the NSPCC; playing snooker; borrowing a telephone; walking in pitch darkness by the canal; our ride on the Tappenham Omnibus; a night of horror; the hilarity of the fire-alarm incident, and conversations with Peter and Elizabeth. I turned again to Aaron as the car drew out of the hostel grounds.

"You really missed a wonderful trip, you know."

"Did you get a good night's sleep then?" came his riposte.

That wiped the grin off my face and he smiled.

"I'd rather not talk about that bit," I admitted.

"Tell me the details later," said Aaron, who clearly wanted to concentrate on driving us home safely.

That suited me. Apart from anything else it was impossible to compete with the noise coming from the back seat. Barney had found his joke book and was doing his best to read out the jokes to his mates. Even when he slipped up on a word or phrase the result was funnier than the original joke. They shrieked with laughter, and I joined in. Aaron just raised his eyes heaven-wards. He doesn't share my childish sense of humour but I was definitely enjoying the back-seat conversation better than he was. That was probably why I enjoyed the boys' company so much – we laughed at the same things.

"*Doctor, doctor, my hair keeps falling out. Can you give me something to keep it in?*"

"*You could try this carrier bag!*" We roared. Then came the next one.

"*Did you hear about the plastic surgeon?*"

"*No, I didn't. Tell me about the plastic surgeon.*"

"*He sat in front of the fire and melted!*"

We hooted and, laughing at one another's laughter, we laughed more.

When he had controlled himself, Barney tried another one.

"*What did the first mind reader say to the second mind reader?*"

"*I don't know. What did the first mind reader say to the second mind reader?*"

"*You're OK. How am I?*"

Silence. We were all trying to work that one out. Then the penny dropped and the boys began to chortle again. I did not. The punch-line of this joke really set me thinking.

"*You're OK. How am I?*"

What a commendable attitude, I thought, and one from which all humankind could benefit, especially we ASSes as we interact with our ADDer counterparts. "**You're** OK. How am I?"

∞ ∞ ∞

Yes, ADDers are OK. Although George Still back in 1902 described children with ADHD as displaying a major, chronic 'defect in moral control', could it really be claimed now, with the greater knowledge that we have, that ADDers really are morally different to ASSes? Is it reasonable to accuse ADDers of being inherently more evil, more devilish creatures with 'bigger horns' than the rest of us? I don't think so. When Barney was a baby, before he became mobile, he was gorgeous. His eyes twinkled and he smiled wickedly. He was a real heart-stopper, and he was universally accepted.

When he became mobile he had just the same character as before; the only difference was that he could move. The way in which he expressed this mobility cannot reasonably be criticised on moral grounds, but it provoked disapproval, if not wrath. Barney was affected by everyone's response to him. The more we tried to discipline him for his antics, the worse his morality appeared to be. We didn't know then about his ADHD or its underlying causes. As time went on and Barney experienced increasing blame and disapprobation, the boundary between his lack of physical control and lack of moral control became more blurred.

ADDers are not fundamentally different from ASSes in this regard. The difference is one of degree rather than kind. In our society they are neurologically disadvantaged. Their frustration, fear and sense of failure, coupled with an understandable inner rage stemming from the injustices they suffer, provoke them to a degree above and beyond what most ASSes ever experience. And who is to be blamed – the antisocial ADDer or the censorious ASSes who drove him to this state? If the ASSes had no idea of the existence of ADHD, it is certainly unfair to condemn them. But what about the situation where a parent, carer, teacher or social worker is informed about ADHD but does not act on this information?

There are three main enemies to the compassionate and just treatment of the ADDer child – ignorance, fear and pride.

Firstly, ignorance. Unless adults are as well-informed about the condition as possible, then we can never respond appropriately.

Secondly, pride. Unless we are prepared to admit that we misjudge ADDer children repeatedly, to apologise where necessary, and try to do better, we will never gain their confidence.

Thirdly, fear. Unless we take courage and face the challenge these children offer we can never help them.

We are all, ASSes and ADDers alike, crazy mixed up kids. On the one hand, chronic failures, and on the other hand glorious beings with a 'divine' spark – a curious mixture of Ape and Angel. None of us is perfect. All of us are fallen creatures, affected by what is known in the Judeo-Christian tradition as Original Sin. St Paul wrote nearly 2000 years ago "*all have sinned and all fall short of the glory of God*"[60] – his way of expressing the universality of the human condition, whether we are male or female, black or white, ADDer or ASS.

The concept of original sin implies that human nature is fallen and we are from birth, if not conception, selfish and rebellious. Imagine a newly born lion, suckling at the teats of the lioness. Is he a carnivore, or is he not? Does he have to eat his first meat meal before he becomes a carnivore, or is he already one? Is it just a matter of semantics? If forced to classify the cub I would say "Yes, he is a carnivore, just like his parents." After all, if in his weaned state he were to be offered a nice juicy steak, he's hardly likely to turn his nose up and say "No thanks! I'm a vegetarian." Being a carnivore is inherent in his nature, independent of the availability of meat.

In the same way, human beings are 'sinners' in the sense that we have sinful natures which are independent of our opportunity to sin. It seems harsh to label a new-born baby as a 'sinner', but this description can be justified as long as we understand that this simply means the infant has a 'me-first' attitude from the very start. What a thought – all babies are 'babies with attitude'! What infant, after all, ever had to be taught selfishness? It is not long before his or her innate egoism becomes obvious.

Then there is the other side of human nature – our glorious side. We may '*fall short of the glory of God*' but we do have something of the glory of God. We are said to be made '*in the image of God*'[61] even if the image has become marred.[62] In fact, the very concept of 'Human Rights' owes its existence to humankind's implicit or explicit belief in this truth. Archbishop Desmond Tutu acknowledges the divine aspect of our being when he writes "*We are temples of the Holy Spirit.*[63] *We are God-carriers and ought to genuflect to one another as we do to the reserved sacrament in the tabernacle*".[64] This is no less true of an ADDer than an ASS.

Delightful and glorious though our Barney and other children with ADHD may be, it cannot be denied that they are very, very difficult to bring up and live with. Parenting such a child hurts. He truly can seem like a 'thorn in the flesh' whose presence is irritating and painful, and many a time I have longed for release while continuing to love him passionately. His own nature is not easy for him either. He fights inner battles, the likes of which I will probably never know. He is his own 'thorn in the flesh', best expressed to me in those moments when he has said "Mummy, I wish I didn't have ADHD."

Of all things 'thorny' in nature, what better can a child with ADHD be compared with than to an immature, pre-blooming rose? Imagine coming across such a plant for the very first time ever. You have never seen a rose at any stage in its life-cycle before now. You barely know that these particular botanical specimens exist, let us say. What you see is most unpromising. It is all green, rather uninteresting, apart from the spikes which flank the stem. They certainly attract your attention, though not your approval. The thorns look particularly uninviting and, if you get too involved, will cause you pain. Your reaction then is to make an angry noise and withdraw as rapidly as possible. You hardly notice the tiny green bud at the top of the plant. Its significance passes you by. There seems to be no reason why you shouldn't consign this weed to the compost heap.

But wait! Consider what might happen if a friend persuaded you to have faith, to take this plant to your heart, to feed it, nurture it, learn to understand even its most complex needs and give it love? In time, that insignificant green blob at the top starts to open and you have the first inklings of its hidden beauty as the petals begin to emerge. You are encouraged, and tend it all the more carefully. Gradually more and more of the bloom appears. How could something which seemed to have had such little potential in its earlier stages now be looking like this? In the fullness of time the entire rose unfurls, and its true splendour is revealed There is hardly a more beautiful sight in the whole garden.

And so it is with the child who has ADHD. Given love, care and nurture – believing that the best is still to come – this unpromising thorny little monster can grow into something wonderful beyond anyone's wildest dream. Nevertheless, it is true: '*There is no gathering of the rose without being pricked by the thorns.*'

∞ ∞ ∞

Another outburst of laughter from the back seat rent the air.

"Not so loud, you lot!" Aaron shouted to make himself heard over the noise of the engine and the boys themselves.

How was it that I got on so well with these young lads? Why did I feel such a close bond with them? A motley rabble we four certainly had been but, I realised, we all had one very significant thing in common. We had all at some time or other experienced discrimination on account of our genes. In my case it was because I am female; in Lee's case because he is black; in Barney and Adam's because they have ADHD.

It is true that as my life has progressed, discrimination towards women has diminished. Unlike my grandmother I have, throughout my adult life, had 'the vote' but there have been many situations in which I have had to face blatant sexism. When I wanted to apply to Cambridge University like my brother, whereas he had a choice of 20 men's colleges, there were only three women's colleges for me to choose from.

A few years later I had graduated and with two Master's degrees behind me I applied to work abroad with VSO (Voluntary Service Overseas). There was a vacant position which would involve a certain amount of work in the field, for which I was well qualified. Although I had no difficulty passing the interview and obtaining references which confirmed my suitability for both the work itself and my ability to cope overseas, I was turned down for the post because I was not male. I can still feel the pain and indignity of having that opportunity thwarted.

Then there was Lee, my little friend of West Indian origin. Lee recounts with furrowed brow the taunts he suffered at lower school where he was called a 'burnt sausage'. In middle school he has been set upon by a gang of white boys, punched and called 'nigger'. He perceives himself to have been ignored and overlooked by the teacher time and again in the classroom when he has been eager to answer a question or discuss a novel idea. He relates this to his skin colour.

And lastly, Barney and Adam – despised and discriminated against both socially and educationally, in the many ways already described, on account of their ADHD.

Emmeline Pankhurst and Germaine Greer have fought for me. Martin Luther King, Nelson Mandela and Desmond Tutu have fought for Lee. But who will stand up for Adam, Barney and their kind? I'll try, but it is a huge task. Fortunately, I am not alone. ADD Information Services (ADDISS [65]) and many support groups and dedicated individuals do a fantastic job against all the odds, and their influence is growing.

Will anyone else join us? "The harvest is plentiful, but the labourers are few".[66] There is so much more that must be done: so many minds yet to be enlightened, and so many attitudes and systems to be changed. For whether or not our society is guilty of 'institutional racism', it is certainly guilty of institutional ADHD-ism.

Like Martin Luther King:

"*I say to you today, my friends, that in spite of the difficulties and frustrations of the moment, I still have a dream*".[67]

> I have a dream that one day we will live in a country where ADHD is no longer taboo: where it is seen to be as normal a genetic trait as eye-colour; where it evokes no sense of peculiarity, inferiority or humiliation from the bearers of that condition; where they are able to walk tall, proud of who and what they are.
>
> I have a dream of a world where the parents of children with ADHD are not met with hostility and censoriousness by fellow shoppers when their kids are behaving immaturely and uncontrollably in a supermarket, but with understanding, tolerance and even kindly assistance.
>
> I have a dream of a land where every child with ADHD can be readily and easily diagnosed at an early age, assisted by pro-active parents, doctors and teachers, and then have their individual needs appropriately addressed in every way.
>
> I have a dream of a national education system in which every child, ADDer and ASS alike, is taught in a way that promotes his learning; of a nation where no child is excluded from school because each and every boy and girl finds education exciting and fulfilling.
>
> I have a dream of a nation where the diversity of human kind is embraced; where ADDers and ASSes meet each other 'half way' in situations where one kind could easily be a source of annoyance to the other, rich with mutual understanding, rejoicing together as they both compliment and complement one another.
>
> I have a dream of a country where the most decrepit prisons are razed to the ground for want of inmates, while the better-built are converted into monasteries, youth hostels and sports centres.

> I have a dream of living in a nation whose citizens see beyond the 'thorns' of ADHD and who work together with perseverance and hope towards the gathering of countless resplendent roses.

We crossed straight over the roundabout on the southern outskirts of our home town. I glanced at my watch. We were in good time. We would make it. Aaron changed gear and together we climbed the long, steep hill.

Post Scriptum

Impoverishment

O impoverished parents of compliant kids!
You sit so quietly, calmly and, dare I say, smugly.
Perfect nuclear families, model types.
"Yes, Mum." "No, Dad" polite: well, publicly so.

Then enter us: wall-climbing, noisy creatures we.
Vibrations of growing disapproval surround.

Immoral?	*No.*
Illegal?	*No.*
Dangerous?	*No.*
Destructive?	*No.*

But who are the winners? Who really have the fun?

Yet misunderstanding, condemnation and rejection abound.
We care not, so dare to enjoy and laugh,
Dare to smile at leaden faces.

And one responds!
First a flicker, a softening eye,
A smile returned.

She enters in, and silently passes from her world to ours.

Anna Richards, November 1999

Glossary

Asperger's Syndrome: A mild form of autism; a neurological disorder which results in difficulties in social skills and obsessional behaviour. Sufferers may have a very pedantic way of speaking, and although their expressive language is superficially perfect, they may misinterpret comments in an excessively literal way.

Attachment Disorder: Children without proper care in their earliest years fail to bond with any care-giver and lack the ability to form and maintain loving, intimate relationships. They develop an unusually high level of stress hormones which affect crucial aspects of brain and body development. They grow up lacking in trust that the world is a safe place and that others will take good care of them. They believe that if they do not control their world then they will die.

Conduct Disorder (CD): A condition characterised by destructive behaviour, excessive aggression to people and animals, deceitfulness, theft, plus serious and chronic rule-breaking to a severe degree.

Dyslexia: An inability or significant difficulty in learning to read or spell, due to the presence of a chronic neurological disorder that inhibits a person's ability to recognise and process graphic symbols, in particular those which pertain to language, even though they otherwise exhibit normal intellectual functions.

Five-Staged Approach to Meeting a Child's Needs:

Stage 1: The lowest stage, and where a child is usually placed initially if he demonstrates a need. Some minimal extra help or an adjustment to his or her environment is provided. If it works within a given time-frame and solves the problem, the child is removed from the register. If matters persist or worsen, then the child would go on to the next stage.

Stage 2: At this stage the SENCO should talk to the child's parents and all his/her teachers and draw up an individual education plan (IEP).

Stage 3: At Stage 3 the SENCO continues to take a leading role and can call in the help of outside agencies – external specialist services relevant to the child's needs, e.g. an educational psychologist or specialist teacher. There may also be a new IEP and the child's parents should always be informed of the action which the school proposes. If the child fails to progress as hoped, then the headteacher, on the advice of the SENCO, should consider advising the LEA that a statutory assessment might be necessary.

Stage 4: Focuses on the statutory assessment of the child's special educational needs. Firstly, it involves the LEA co-operating with the child's school and parents and, if appropriate, other agencies to consider whether a statutory assessment is necessary. Secondly, it conducts that assessment if it is deemed necessary, again working co-operatively with parents, school and other agencies.

Stage 5: When the results of a statutory assessment indicate that the child needs special help which cannot reasonably be provided within the resources normally available to the school – resources such as money, staff time and special equipment – a document called a Statement of Special Educational Needs is drawn up and sets out the child's needs and all the special help which he or she should have.

Learning Support Assistant: An assistant who provides in-school support for pupils with special educational needs and/or disabilities. An LSA normally provides a particular pupil or pupils with close support and assists those responsible for teaching him/her.

Named Person: Someone who assists the child's parents to express their views and who offers them advice, information and personal support whenever needed. He or she may be appointed at any time during the special needs identification process and can attend all meetings with the parents. The Named Person should be independent of the LEA and may be a personal friend or someone from a voluntary organisation or parent partnership scheme.

Note in Lieu of a Statement: This is a document issued to the child's parents and school which sets out the reasons for the LEA's decision not to make a statement. The parents should be sent copies of all the advice which the LEA obtained from the professionals to whom they spoke during the statutory assessment. The note and that advice should elucidate the LEA's decision and can be passed to the school to help the child's teachers decide how to help him or her in the future.

Obsessive Compulsive Disorder (OCD): A spectrum of symptoms characterised by obsessions and compulsions which in the extreme cases can be quite incapacitating. Bedrooms may have to be organised in a fastidious way; specific cutlery and crockery may be demanded at mealtimes; household items may have to be positioned at all times in a specific location. Someone with OCD may also like and need routines or indulge in compulsive hand-washing or some other act of cleanliness. If the carrying out of their obsession or compulsion is thwarted, it may lead to significant defiance, tantrums and behavioural upsets which can be mistaken for Oppositional Defiant Disorder.

Oppositional Defiant Disorder (ODD): Children with ODD regularly lose their temper, are excessively hostile, argue with adults, refuse to comply and deliberately annoy others. They are frequently very touchy and easily annoyed; excessively angry and resentful; spiteful and vindictive; and blame everything and everyone else for their mistakes and failures

Post-Traumatic Stress Disorder (PTSD): One of the enduring consequences of traumatic experiences. PTSD has been identified throughout recorded human history. Today PTSD can be found across genders, cultures, and socio-economic groups and may result from the experience of war, vehicle accidents, sexual abuse and violence, for example.

SMART Targets:

Small: If the target is too big to be achieved in a reasonable length of time, motivation is lost. Small can be achieved by being specific.

Measurable: "How will I know if the target has been achieved?" If the answer is "Don't know!", then the target is not measurable.

Accessible: The pupil must be able to engage with the target. It must be at the right level. If they can't do it, it's not too easy.

Realistic: The target must be achievable in terms of available resources. Resources include time and personnel.

Timed: A time for achieving the target should be set and review held when that time is up. All those involved, including the pupil, should be aware of the time set and the review date.

Special Educational Needs Co-ordinator (SENCO): a member of staff who has responsibility for co-ordinating the provision of special educational needs within a school. In small schools the headteacher or deputy may take on this role, while in larger schools there may be a special educational needs co-ordinating team.

Statement of Special Educational Needs: Otherwise known simply as a 'statement'. See Stage 5 of the five-staged approach, above.

Tourette's Syndrome: A neurological disorder typified by the presence of persistent multiple vocal and motor tics which occur in bouts and cause significant distress or impairment in social, occupational or other areas of functioning.

Appendix 1

Some reasons against educating Barney at home:

- The child cannot benefit from the example set by peers.
- The child is vulnerable to the absence of the class teacher.
- It is impossible for a child to play team sports alone.
- There can be stresses when the child and home teacher are together all the time.
- It is difficult to learn social skills without a peer group.

Appendix 2

Form Provided by our LEA for the SENCO

Type of Learning Difficulty: (Please tick appropriate box)

Moderate Learning Difficulties	☐
Specific Learning Difficulties (including dyslexia and dyspraxia)	☐
Emotional and Behavioural Difficulties	☐
Physical Disability	☐
Hearing Impairment	☐
Visual Impairment	☐
Deaf/Blind Impairment	☐
Communication Difficulties (including Autism, Asperger's Syndrome, speech and language difficulties)	☐
Severe Learning Difficulties	☐

Appendix 3

While the strategies listed here are perfectly sound in themselves, the sheer lengths of the lists may possibly make a mainstream schoolteacher feel overwhelmed.

This appendix has been extracted from ADHD Information and Guidelines for Schools, *published by Hampshire County Council Education Department, December 1996, and is reprinted here with the kind permission of Cliff Turner, Assessment & Intervention Manager (Principal Educational Psychologist).*

A: Classroom Management Strategies for AD(H)D Pupils

1. Physical arrangement of the classroom

Use rows for tasks which do not require interpersonal contact. Avoid the use of tables with groups of pupils, as this maximises interpersonal distractions for the AD(H)D pupil.

Ideally a classroom should provide flexibility of seating, with several tables for group work and rows for independent work.

Arranging desks in a horseshoe shape has been found to promote discussion without impeding independent work.

Sit distractible pupils near the teacher – as close as possible without being perceived as punitive.

Locate the more distractible pupils away from windows and corridors to minimise visual and auditory distractions.

Keep a part of the room free from obvious visual and auditory distracters.

Seat peer models with good study skills next to children showing attentional difficulties and over-activity.

2. Lesson organisation

Provide an outline, key concepts and essential vocabulary prior to lesson or topic presentation.

Vary the pace of lesson presentation.

Include a variety of activities during each lesson.

When appropriate, intersperse in-seat tasks with more physical activities.

Use multisensory presentation, but make sure that interesting pictures and sounds relate directly to the material to be learned.

Set short achievable targets and reward task completion promptly. Allow a short break before the next target is set.

Actively involve pupils in lesson preparation.

Encourage pupils to develop mental images of the concepts or information being presented. Ask them about their images to be sure they are visualising the key material to be learned.

Use co-operative learning activities, particularly those that assign each child in a group a specific role or piece of information that is needed to complete the group task.

3. General organisation

Establish a daily classroom schedule and ensure that routines are known and practised, particularly for beginnings, endings and transitions.

Give five minute warning before ending of a session for the completion of the task and putting away equipment etc.

Use individual assignment charts or home-school book to go home with the pupil and be signed daily by the parent if necessary.

Be clear about when pupil movement is permitted, when it is not allowed and when it is discouraged.

Use a kitchen timer to indicate special periods of intense independent work and reinforce the class for appropriate behaviour during this period. Start with briefer periods (five to 10 minutes) and gradually increase the length of time as the class develops success.

4. Behaviour

Keep classroom rules simple and clear, with examples of keeping and breaking the rule modelled and role-played.

Actively reinforce desired classroom behaviours.

Praise specific behaviour. For example: "I like how you correctly wrote down all the things you have to do" rather than "Well done!"

Frequently move about the room so that you can maximise your degree of proximity control.

Set short measurable goals for behaviour with lesson by lesson reinforcement.

Tackle only one target behaviour at a time.

B: Strategies to Address Specific Behavioural Issues of Individual Pupils

1. Inattention

Provide frequent, immediate and consistent feedback on behaviour and redirection back to task.

Seat pupil in a quiet area.

Seat pupil near a good role model.

Increase distance between desks.

Seat pupil away from distracting stimuli.

Give assignments one at a time.

Include a variety of activities during each lesson.

Assist pupil in setting short-term goals.

Restrict homework to that which is essential.

Give clear, concise instructions.

Provide written outline of lesson.

Cue pupil to stay on task, e.g. using a private signal.

Let pupil share recently learned concepts etc. with a peer still having difficulty with them.

Pay careful attention to design of worksheets and tests.

Use large type and provide only one or two activities per page.

Keep page format simple.

Avoid extraneous pictures or visual distracters that are not specifically and directly related to the task.

Have white space on each page.

Use dark black print and avoid hand-written worksheets or tests if possible.

Write clear, simple directions.

Provide alternative environments with fewer distractions for taking tests.

Allow pupil to use tape recorder sometimes rather than always requiring written work.

Shorten assignments. If the pupil can demonstrate adequate skill mastery in 10 or 20 questions, don't require completion of 30 or 40 items.

2. Excessive motor activity

Choose the AD(H)D pupil to be the one who writes keywords or ideas on the board, etc.

Allow opportunities for pupil to move around the room.

Provide short breaks between assignments.

Remind pupil to check work if performance is rushed or careless.

Plan ahead for transitions. Establish rules and supervise closely.

3. Poor organisation and planning

Establish a daily classroom routine and schedule.

Organise desks and folders daily. Check for neatness.

Persuade parents to use organiser trays at home marked with the day or the week so that books and work required at school that day are all together.

A personal visual timetable may be helpful in view of the difficulty with time concepts.

Fasten a checklist to the pupil's desk, or put one in each subject folder/exercise book to outline the steps to be taken in following directions or checking to ensure that a task is correctly completed.

Give notes to the pupil about key elements in the lesson.

Use individual homework assignment charts that can be seen and signed by parents.

Provide rules for getting organised.

Give assignments one at a time.

Supervise recording of homework assignments.

Check homework daily.

Assist pupil in short-term goals in completing assignments.

4. Impulsiveness

Keep classroom rules clear and simple

Ignore minor inappropriate behaviour.

Increase immediate rewards and consequences.

Use careful reprimands for misbehaviour (criticise the behaviour not the child).

Attend to positive behaviour with compliments.

Seat pupil near a good role model or near teacher.

Encourage the pupil to verbalise what must be done: aloud to the teacher in a one to one setting at first, then whispering quietly to self and finally saying silently to self.

Teach verbal mediation skills to reduce impulsive behaviour by modelling. Practise a structured routine of stop/listen, look/think, answer/do.

5. Non-compliance

Praise compliant behaviour.

Provide immediate feedback about acceptable and unacceptable behaviour.

Use teacher attention to reinforce positive behaviour.

6. Difficulties with peers

Praise appropriate social behaviour.

Organise social skills training to teach concepts of communication, participation and co-operation.

Define social behavioural goals with pupil and implement a reward programme.

Encourage co-operative learning tasks with other pupils.

Praise pupil frequently to increase esteem within the classroom.

Assign special responsibilities to pupil in presence of peer group so others observe pupil in a positive light.

7. Poor self-esteem

Provide reassurance and encouragement.

Frequently compliment positive behaviour.

Focus on pupil's talents and accomplishments.

Reinforce frequently when signs of frustration are noticed.

Appendix 4

Some reasons against placing a Learning Support Assistant (LSA) alongside every child with ADHD throughout his/her education:

- It is financially inefficient.
- It continually draws attention to the child's differences.
- The gender issue – most children with diagnosed ADHD are male: most LSAs are female.
- The low rate of pay predisposes LSAs to low expertise, particularly with complex conditions such as ADHD.
- LSAs cannot change the curriculum to suit the child.
- LSAs are not usually trained in special teaching methods to suit the child.

Appendix 5

Effective methods for teaching children with ADHD

- Use drama and role-play in any curriculum subject.
- Provide the opportunity to engage with learning matter through tactile or kinaesthetic means.
- 'Catching them being good' and give much praise, ignoring negative behaviour if possible, otherwise dealing with it as unobtrusively as possible.
- Repeat daily patterns of lessons – break down tasks and activities into a few sub-tasks and activities.
- Give frequent and specific feedback, with small and immediate rewards which should be child-specific and negotiated with the pupil.
- Avoid putting children with ADHD in group situations, but rather use pairs.

Appendix 6

Methods of detecting/assessing/diagnosing ADHD:

- Radioactive glucose input and Positron Emission Tomography (PET) scanning of brain.
- Dopamine uptake measurement.
- Push button tests linked to measurement of blood flow in the brain via functional Magnetic Resonance Imaging (fMRI).
- Conners' Continuous Performance Test.
- DSM-IV Criteria for ADHD (Diagnostic and Statistical Manual of Mental Disorders, Fourth Edition).

Appendix 7

This appendix contains the most frequently used method for diagnosing AD/HD at present.

Diagnostic and Statistical Manual of Mental Disorders Fourth Edition 1994 (DSM-IV™)

Diagnostic Criteria for Attention-Deficit/Hyperactivity Disorder (AD/HD) *

A. Either (1) or (2)

(1) Six (or more) of the following symptoms of inattention have persisted for at least six months to a degree that is maladaptive and inconsistent with development level:

Inattention

a) Often fails to give close attention to details or makes careless mistakes in schoolwork, work or other activities.

b) Often has difficulty sustaining attention in tasks or play activities.

c) Often does not seem to listen when spoken to directly.

d) Often does not follow through on instructions and fails to finish schoolwork, chores or duties in the workplace (not due to oppositional behaviour or failure to understand instructions).

e) Often has difficulty organising tasks and activities.

f) Often avoids, dislikes or is reluctant to engage in tasks that require sustained mental effort (such as schoolwork or homework).

g) Often loses things necessary for tasks or activities (e.g. toys, school assignments, pencils, books or tools).

h) Is often easily distracted by extraneous stimuli.

i) Is often forgetful in daily activities.

(2) Six (or more) of the following symptoms of hyperactivity-impulsivity have persisted for at least six months to a degree that is maladaptive and inconsistent with developmental level:

Hyperactivity

a) Often fidgets with hands or feet or squirms in seat.

b) Often leaves seat in classroom or in other situations in which remaining seated is expected.

c) Often runs about or climbs excessively in situations in which it is inappropriate (in adolescents or adults, may be limited to subjective feelings of restlessness).

d) Often has difficulty playing or engaging in leisure activities quietly.

e) Is often 'on the go' or often acts as if 'driven by a motor'.

f) Often talks excessively.

Impulsivity

g) Often blurts out answers before questions have been completed.

h) Often has difficulty awaiting turn.

i) Often interrupts or intrudes on others (e.g. butts into conversations or games).

B. Some hyperactive-impulsive or inattentive symptoms that caused impairment were present before the age of seven years.

C. Some impairment from the symptoms is present in two or more settings (e.g., at school (or work) and at home).

D. There must be clear evidence of clinically significant impairment in social, academic or occupational functioning.

E. The symptoms do not occur exclusively during the course of a Pervasive Developmental Disorder, Schizophrenia, or other Psychotic Disorder, and are not better accounted for by another mental disorder (e.g. Mood Disorder, Anxiety Disorder, Dissociative Disorder or a Personality Disorder).

Code based on type:

314.01 Attention-Deficit/Hyperactivity Disorder, Combined Type: If both Criteria A1 and A2 are met for the past 6 months.

314.00 Attention-Deficit/Hyperactivity Disorder, Predominantly Inattentive Type: if Criterion A1 is met but Criterion A2 is not met for the past six months.

314.01 Attention-Deficit/Hyperactivity Disorder, Predominantly Hyperactive – Impulsive Type: If Criterion A2 is met but Criterion A1 is not met for the past six months.

Coding Note: For individuals (especially adolescents and adults) who currently have symptoms that no longer meet full criteria, "In Partial Remission" should be specified.

**** Reprinted with permission from the Diagnostic and Statistical Manual of Mental Disorders, Fourth Edition. Copyright 1994 American Psychiatric Association.***

References

1. Kewley, G.D. (1995) 'Medical Aspects of Assessment and Treatment of Children with Attention Deficit Disorder', in Cooper, P. and Ideus, K. (eds) ADHD: Educational, Medical and Cultural Issues. Association of Workers for Children with Emotional and Behavioural Difficulties (AWCEBD) Publishers.
2. Howard Hughes Medical Institute News. (1999) 'Serotonin May Hold Key to Hyperactivity-Disorder Disorder Treatment', 15th January. (Internet).
3. Goddard, Sally. (1996) 'A Teacher's Window into the Child's Mind' p88. Fern Ridge Press.
4. Kewley, G.D. (1999) Attention Deficit Hyperactivity Disorder: Recognition, Reality and Resolution pp58,59. Learning Assessment Centre (LAC) Press.
5. Bloch, H. (1994) 'Life in Overdrive', Time magazine 18 July, 46.
6. Kewley, G.D. (1997, April) 'Attention Deficit Hyperactivity Disorder', Notes from the Learning Assessment Centre, Horsham, West Sussex, RH12 2PD.
7. LADDER (National Learning and Attention Deficit Disorders Association) (1994) Factsheet,.
8. Kannemann, F. (1993) 'What is Attention Deficit Disorder' in Frequently Asked Questions from the Net, p1. (Internet).
9. Novartis (UK) Ltd. (1998) ADHD - A Guide for Parents and Guardians, p3.
10. Hartmann, T. (1999) ADD - A Different Perception, p10. Newleaf.
11. Home Office, (1995) Criminal Statistics England and Wales, 1994. London: HMSO.
12. Hartmann, T. (1999) ADD - A Different Perception, p7. Newleaf.
13. Martin, C. (1979) A Short History of English Schools, pp97-99. Wayland.
14. Kewley, G.D (1999). Attention Deficit Hyperactivity Disorder: Recognition, Reality and Resolution, p142. Learning Assessment Centre (LAC) Press.
15. See Appendix 1.
16. For further information on coaching contact 'The Coaching Centre UK, 13 Upper Addison Gardens, London W14 8AP. Tel: 0207 603 0368. Fax: 0171 603 5359. E mail: DZaccheo@aol.com'
17. Multimodal Treatment of ADHD (MTA) Cooperative Group. (1999) 'A 14-month Randomized Clinical Trial of Treatment Strategies for Attention Deficit Hyperactivity Disorder', Archives of Geneneral Psychiatry 56:1073-86.
18. Holy Bible. Ecclesiastes 1:9.
19. Cooper, P. and Ideus, K. (1996) ADHD A Practical Guide for Teachers, p37. David Fulton Publishers.
20. ADDNet Team (compiled from various sources) (1999). Article in AD/HD Support Group North East News Magazine, July.
21. Goddard, Sally. (1996) 'A Teacher's Window into the Child's Mind' p90. Fern Ridge Press.
22. Lewis, C.S. (1960) The Four Loves, Chapter 5. Geoffrey Bles Ltd.
23. ADDNet Team (compiled from various sources) (1999). Article in AD/HD Support Group North East News Magazine, July.
24. Contact Dr Roy Eskapa at the London Enuresis Clinic, FREEPOST SW7186, LONDON, SW6 4YY, UK. Tel: 0207 371 8553. Email: rde@bedwet.com
25. Martin, C. (1979) A Short History of English Schools, p63. Wayland.
26. Ibid. p 49.
27. See Appendix 2.
28. van der Post, L. (1964) Journey Into Russia, Chapter 4. Hogarth Press.
29. Cooper, P. and Ideus, K. (1996) ADHD: A Practical Guide for Teachers, p17. David Fulton Publishers.
30. Ibid. p 9.
31. Kewley, G.D. (1995) 'Medical Aspects of Assessment and Treatment of Children with Attention Deficit Disorder', in Cooper, P. and Ideus, K. (eds.) ADHD: Educational, Medical and Cultural Issues. Association of Workers for Children with Emotional and Behavioural Difficulties (AWCEBD) Publishers.
32. McCann, J.B. et al. (1996) 'Prevalence of Psychiatric Disorders in Young People in the Care System', British Medical Journal 313:1529-1530.
33. Kendall, J. (1999) "Sibling Accounts of ADHD". Family Process magazine, 38, pp117-136.

34. Fein, Aubrey and Joyce (1998) At the Crossroads, p 130. A. Fein Publishing. (Copies of this book may be obtained from ADD Information Services, P O Box 340, Edgware, HA8 9HL, Tel: 0208 905 2013, Fax: 0208 386 6466, e-mail addiss@compuserve.com)
35. See Appendix 3.
36. Kewley, G. D. (1997) 'Attention Deficit Hyperactivity Disorder', Notes from the Learning Assessment Centre, April.
37. Holy Bible. Romans 12:2 (J B Phillips' Translation).
38. Barkley, R. (1990) ADHD: A Handbook for Diagnosis and Treatment. Guilford Press.
39. Biederman, J. et al. (1999) 'Pharmacotherapy of ADHD Reduces Risk for Substance Use Disorder', Pediatrics Vol.104 No 2.
40. The Royal College of Psychiatrists (1999) 'Stimulant Medication for Hyperkinetic Disorder and ADHD', Factsheet 6 for Parents and Teachers.
41. See Appendix 4.
42. Cruickshank, W. M. 'A New Perspective in Teacher Education: The Neuroeducator.' Journal of Learning Disabilities 14:337-341 and 367.
43. See Appendix 5. (From Cooper, P. and Ideus, K. (1996) ADHD: A Practical Guide for Teachers. David Fulton Publishers).
44. Sanford, J. HM Prison Officer (1998) Lecture given at the 2nd Annual ADD Information Services Conference, London, October 1998.
45. See Appendix 6.
46. Chandan, J. V. et al. (1998) 'Selective Effects of Methylphenidate in ADHD: A Functional Magnetic Resonance Study', Proceedings of the National Academy of Sciences Vol.95, Issue 24, 14494-14499.
47. See Appendix. 7.
48. Holy Bible. John 14:15.
49. Holy Bible. Romans 6:16,17.
50. Holy Bible. John 8:34.
51. Martin, C. (1979) A Short History of English Schools p73, Wayland.
52. Hartmann, T. (1999) ADD - A Different Perception p134 ff, Newleaf.
53. Martin, C. (1979) A Short History of English Schools p48, Wayland.
54. Horn, P. (1989) The Victorian and Edwardian Schoolchild p23, Alan Sutton.
55. Rosen, B. (1995) 'State Involvement in Public Education before the 1870 Education Act', The Victorian Web, (from the Internet).
56. Rosen, B. ibid.
57. Martin, C. (1979) A Short History of English Schools p46, Wayland.
58. Cooper, P. and Ideus, K. (1996) ADHD: A Practical Guide for Teachers p77, David Fulton Publishers.
59. Kewley, G.D. (1997) Notes on ADHD, Published by The Learning Assessment Centre, April 1997.
60. Holy Bible. Romans 3:23.
61. Holy Bible. Genesis 1:27.
62. Holy Bible. Genesis Chapter 3.
63. Holy Bible. 1Corinthians 6:19.
64. Tutu, D. (1984) Hope and Suffering p60, Fount Paperbacks.
65. ADDISS, 10 Station Road, Mill Hill Broadway, London NW7 2JU, Tel. 020 8906 9068 e-mail: info@addiss.co.uk website: www.addiss.co.uk
66. Holy Bible. Matthew 9:37.
67. King Jr., Martin Luther (1963) Speech delivered on the steps at the Lincoln Memorial in Washington DC, 28th August 1963.

Index